'S COLL OF EDUCATION

Threshold to Music

SECOND EDITION

Level One Teacher's Resource Book

ELEANOR KIDD
MUSIC CONSULTANT
Richmond, California

PITMAN LEARNING, INC.
Belmont, California

Acknowledgments

Credit and grateful appreciation are due the publishers and owners for use of the following songs. Any omissions are due to the difficulty in finding the source of the material and can be corrected by contacting Fearon Publishers, Belmont, California.

"Little Ducklings" and "Old Woman" from *Exploring Music, Books Two and Three,* by Eunice Boardman and Beth Landis, Holt, Rinehart and Winston, Inc., 1966.

"Camptown Races," Stephen Foster, from *Discovering Music Together, Books Three and Four,* by Beatrice Perham Krone, Charles Leonard, Irving Wolfe, and Margaret Fullerton. Copyright © 1966, 1973 by Follett Educational Corporation, division of Follett Corporation. Used by permission.

"We're Going Round the Mountain" and "Good bye, Old Paint" from *Making Music Your Own, Books Two and Four,* Silver Burdett Company, Division of General Learning Corporation, 1971.

"Hop Old Squirrel" from Dorothy Scarborough, *On the Trail of Negro Folksongs,* Cambridge, Mass.: Harvard University Press, Copyright 1925 by Harvard University Press, 1953 by Harvard University Press, 1953 by Mary McDaniel Parker; used by permission.

"Brooms" from *The Ditty Bag* compiled by Janet Tobitt, used by permission.

Appreciation and thanks are also given to the teachers and pupils of the Richmond Unified School District, California, for their cooperation and whole-hearted enthusiasm in proving many of the concepts presented in this book. Thanks, also, to Julie Kranhold for her never-ending patience.

Cover Art: "Dog Barking at the Moon" by Joan Miro (Oil on Canvas, 1926). Reproduced by permission of the Philadelphia Museum of Art; the A. E. Gallatin Collection; Photo by Alfred J. Wyatt.

Edited and Designed by Julie Kranhold
Illustrated by Hildy Burns and Darcy Paige
Photographs by John Monroe

Foreword

Recent years have generated new insights concerning purposes and methods of music education. One of the major thrusts has been toward the totality of music education with special attention to music as it is heard, felt, imagined, and created. The aural nature of music is being placed once again in the center of the music experience. The development of aural acuity becomes the basis for improved performance, improvisation, and creative activities.

The *Threshold to Music, Second Edition,* exemplifies this contemporary emphasis in teaching music to children. Rhythmic comprehension, melodic contour, feeling for phrasing, and dynamics and pitch contrast are all approached through the ear and body movement.

Visual matters are presented only after aural recognition and body response have provided a foundation for musical learning. Inner hearing, seeing what one hears, and hearing what one sees are integral features of the lessons presented.

The program proceeds in sequential fashion, and lessons are carefully outlined in a way that makes them very attractive to classroom teachers who need such support to build confidence in teaching their own music. One of the outstanding features is the use of charts instead of books, making it possible for the teacher to pinpoint class attention on the concepts presented. Without concentrated eye involvement with the score as music is heard, studied, and sung, music reading ability will not develop. Thus, the use of such charts helps to overcome one of the weaknesses of much music teaching, and raises the level of music literacy.

KARL D. ERNST
Past President International Society for Music Education
Past President Music Educators National Conference
Past Professor Music Education, California State University, Hayward

Musical Terms

Accelerando Becoming faster.

Accent The stress of one tone over others, usually on the first beat.

Anacrusis Up beat or pickpup which indicates a melody begins with an incomplete measure.

Andante A slow even tempo; Italian for "going."

Beat The basic unit of time in music, usually organized in groups of two or three.

Cadence A musical resting place at the end of a phrase or section of a composition.

Chord A simultaneous sounding of three or more tones.

Crescendo A gradual increase in volume of sound indicated by the sign <.

DaCapo Repeat the music from the beginning to the end. Abbreviated to D.C. and meaning "from the beginning."

Diatonic The order of notes as found on the white keys of the piano, using whole steps and half-steps.

Decrescendo A gradual decrease in volume of sound indicated by the sign >.

Dynamics Varying and contrasting degrees of intensity or loudness.

Eighth note A unit of musical notation that receives one-half the time value of the quarter note (♪).

Fine The end in Italian, pronounced "fee-nay." The term to indicate the end of a composition.

Form The organization of all elements of a composition to achieve aesthetic logic.

Forte Italian word meaning loud and strong, abbreviated to *f*.

Fortissimo Very loud, abbreviated to *ff*.

Half-note The half-note receives half the value of a whole note and receives two pulses when the lower number of the time signature is four (♩).

Half-rest The sign (—) indicating silence corresponding to the half-note.

Inner hearing Hearing the melodic pattern within the body without singing or playing.

Measure The space between two bar lines.

Melodic contour A melody pictured by a line drawing or other notation.

Mezzo Italian for middle or half.

Mystery song Recognition of a familiar song by rhythm pattern.

Octave An interval consisting of eight diatonic notes.

Ostinato Italian, meaning stubborn. A clearly defined musical figure which is persistently repeated, usually by the same voice or pitch.

Pattern A succession of notes which forms a recognizable unit.

Pentatonic A scale of five tones with no half-steps between any two tones. Related to the five black keys on the piano.

Phrase A natural division of the melodic line, comparable to a sentence in speech.

Piano Italian for soft. Indicated by *p*.

Pianissimo Very soft, indicated by *pp*.

Quarter note A unit of notation that receives one pulse when the lower number of the time signature is four (♩).

Quarter rest A sign (𝄽) indicating silence corresponding to the value of a quarter note.

Repeat signs A sign signifying that the music between ‖: and :‖ is to be repeated.

Rhythm Notes of different duration combined in sequence to create a pattern.

Rondo A composition characterized by the principle theme being repeated after each new theme is introduced.

Solmization A method of teaching scales and intervals using syllables.

Tempo Italian for time, with regard to speed. Pace at which a composition is to be performed.

Triad A chord of three tones.

Triplet A group of three notes performed in place of two notes of the same value and indicated by a three and a bracket ($\frac{3}{\sqcap}$).

Whole note The largest single unit of modern music notation receiving a value of four pulsations in $\frac{4}{4}$ meter (𝅝).

Whole rest A pause or silence equal in length to a whole note (—).

Contents

Introduction

The second edition of the *Threshold to Music* is greatly influenced by the pedagogy of Zoltán Kodály. In keeping with Professor Kodály's belief that all children should be provided with musical skills, this program will enable the teacher to present a developmental approach to the reading and writing of music.

To the teacher:

who feels that the teaching of music is not one of his or her strengths, either through lack of experience or training, and, therefore, lack of interest,

who has little or no help from a music specialist due to scheduling or financial needs of the school district,

who feels there can be musical experiences other than the conventional "songbook-record" approach,

the *Threshold to Music* will provide a stepping stone to rewarding musical experiences involving singing, music reading, and participation.

The teacher of the self-contained classroom can have the greatest influence on a child's attitude to all learning. The teacher's enthusiasm, sense of humor, intelligence, and training can give the child experiences that cannot be duplicated. It is natural to teach from personal strengths, whether reading, language arts, science, art, physical education, or music. This is the natural desire in all of us—to be successful. Many times this desire leads to imbalance within the educational framework. Therefore, it would be ideal to have a "specialist" come into the classroom and "take over" those subject areas that are not one of the teacher's "strengths," but until that ideal becomes a reality, the classroom teacher must try to be all-knowing in the various programs offered in the schools.

For ease of planning, the *Teacher's Resource Book* contains a miniature of each classroom chart with each lesson. Although it might be a temptation to present the classroom charts at the beginning of each lesson, greater success will be achieved by the utilization of preparatory experiences. Rhythmic and melodic activities should be presented at the beginning of the school year, using familiar songs from previous experiences.

BASIC RHYTHMIC AND MELODIC ACTIVITIES

- Sing many songs—folk songs, nursery rhymes, camp songs, and spirituals.
- Start the day with a song, take a break with a song, create new words to a familiar song.
- Call the daily roll using sol–mi (G to E on the piano); the children will echo their name. For example,

Teacher sings	Mary echoes
Ma–ry	I'm here
(sol) (mi)	(sol) (mi)

- Use rhythmic activities at various times of the day, to relieve tensions, to provide a transition from one subject to another, to teach children to listen and follow directions, and to give children an opportunity for leadership. For example,

Sing a song and *clap* the **beat.**
Sing a song and *step* the **beat.**
Sing a song, *walk* the **beat,** *change direction* at the end of the **phrase.**
Sing a song and *clap* the **pattern** (syllables of the words).
- Build a musical vocabulary through a song to provide the children with experiences that will lead to success when presented with the classroom charts. See the list of "Musical Terms" presented in this book on page 4.

The *Preparation for the Chart* in the *Teacher's Resource Book* may be presented several days prior to introducing the charts to the class.

It will be obvious to those who read the material that each lesson presents more activities than can be accomplished successfully in a single music lesson. The *Other Songs to Use* and *Additional Activities* provide the teacher with a variety of enrichment experiences that will fit the needs and individuality of the children in the classroom.

The second edition of the *Threshold to Music* will enable the classroom teacher to discover the excitement of learning how to learn through music. The involvement of the teacher and child in rhythm and song through the use of the classroom charts will provide musical perception and awareness that can be related to all learning. To understand the potential this program can offer, one need only remember the old Chinese proverb: "He who hears, forgets; he who sees, remembers; but he who does, knows."

E.K.

1

Can You Keep the Beat?

PREPARATION FOR THE CHART

A. HICKORY, DICKORY DOCK

J. W. Elliot   Mother Goose

Hick - o - ry, dick - o - ry dock,   The

mouse   ran up   the clock,   The

clock struck "one,"   the mouse   ran down.

Hick - o - ry, dick - o - ry dock. (tick, tock)

1. Teach the song.
2. Sing the song and clap the **beat** (two beats to a **measure**).
3. Sing the song and step the beat.

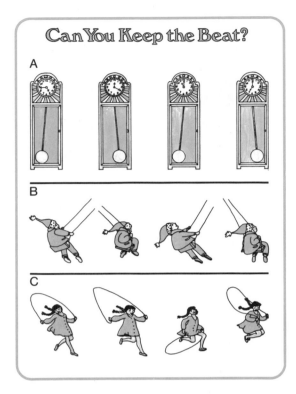

Can You Keep the Beat?

A

B

C

4. Sing the song and walk the beat; at the end of each **phrase** (⌒), change direction (this is called **turning the phrase**).
5. Sing the song and dramatize the words as follows:

   - Phrase 1—make a pendulum with your arms
   - Phrase 2—let the fingers crawl up in the air
   - Phrase 3—make a sign for "one" and let the fingers crawl down
   - Phrase 4—make a pendulum with your arms

6. Sing the song, let the body act as a pendulum, and clap the words (this is called clapping the **pattern**).

B. SWING, SWING

Eleanor Kidd

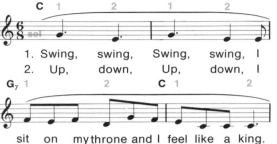

1. Swing,   swing,   Swing,   swing,   I
2. Up,   down,   Up,   down,   I

sit   on   my throne and I feel   like   a   king.
swing down so   low Then I swing up   so high.

Swing,   swing,   Swing,   swing,   Good-
Up,   down,   Up,   down,   I

bye   to   the ground, I'm   a   bird   on the wing.
know   I   will   land   On that cloud in the sky.

1. Teach the song.
2. Sing the song and swing the beat (two beats to a measure). Hold on to an imaginary rope and sway forward and back.
3. Sing the song and hold a partners hands while swinging forward and back.

4. Sing the song, walk the beat with a swaying motion, and swing the arms loosely, alternating right and left (laterality).
5. Repeat the above activity, but this time turn the phrases without losing the beat.

C. JUMPING

Eleanor Kidd

Jump and jump and jump the beat;

Jump-ing, jump-ing go our feet.

Jump up high and jump down low;

Turn a-round and sit just so.

1. Teach the song.
2. Sing the song and clap the beat vigorously (2 claps to a measure).
3. Sing the song and jump the beat.
4. Sing the song, jump the beat, turn around on the sixth measure without losing the beat, and sit down on the last measure.

INTRODUCE THE CHART

[Note: Use the inquiry method.]

1. *Line 1.* What kind of a sound does a grandfather clock make? Is it different from a wrist watch? What is a pendulum? Point to the illustrations and read line 1. Dramatize a clock's pendulum while the children say "tick-tock." What happens when the clock stops? Does it lose the beat?

Line 2. Point to the illustrations on the chart and read Line 2 with "Swing, Swing." Dramatize the motion of swinging while reading the chart and singing the song.

Line 3. Point to the illustrations on the chart. Dramatize jumping rope for the song "Jump." What happens to the beat if you "miss"? Did the beat get lost?

ADDITIONAL ACTIVITIES

1. Use appropriate instruments with each song.

   Line 1—sticks, woodblocks
   Line 2—sandblocks, autoharp (Let one child strum the beat while the teacher presses down the C and G₇ chords.)
   Line 3—sticks, woodblocks, drum

2. Clap the words (pattern) to one of the songs. The child who correctly identifies the song comes up to the chart and keeps the beat while the class sings the song.

3. Choose a child to clap a **mystery song** for the class. (This is done by clapping the word pattern of a song without losing the beat; the class must then guess what the song is.) For example,

   Teddy bear, Teddy bear

   clap-clap clap clap-clap clap

4. Songs like "Swing, Swing" and "Jumping" lend themselves to original verses and activities. For example,

   "Swing, Swing,"
   "Row, Row,"
   "Roll, Roll"

   Let the children create their own words and decide which motion to use. Give

specific instructions for the final **cadence:** "Kneel down," "Bow low," "Turn around."

EVALUATION OF RHYTHMIC AND PERCEPTUAL SKILLS

Psychomotor Development and Perception

1. Can the children keep the beat with their hands, feet, and body.
2. Is their motion relaxed and free? Do their arms swing freely with the beat of the song (laterality)?
3. Can the children turn the phrases while walking or jumping without losing their balance (position in space)?

Aural Acuity and Perception

1. Can the children identify a song by its rhythm pattern?
2. Can the children clap a mystery song for the class to identify?

Visual Acuity and Perception

Can the children follow the figures on the chart while singing, clapping, jumping?

Read the Beat

CLAP YOUR HANDS

U.S. Folksong

Clap, clap, clap your hands,

Clap your hands to - geth - er.

Clap, clap, clap your hands,

Clap your hands to - geth - er.

Read the Beat

PREPARATION FOR THE CHART

1. Teach the song.
2. Sing the song and clap the beat.
3. Create new verses and motions for the song.

- Tap, tap, tap your toe
- Nod, nod, nod your head
- Do, do, do all three
- Walk, walk, walk the beat

4. Sing the song and walk the beat.
5. Sing the song, walk the beat, and turn the phrases (⌒).

6. Sing the song and clap the words (pattern).
7. Sing the song, step the pattern, and clap the beat.

[Note: This activity will have to be repeated several times before all the children are successful. Later try turning the phrases with this activity.]

INTRODUCE THE CHART

1. Point to the beats on the chart while the children clap and say "clap" for each beat, moving from line to line without losing the beat.
2. Clap the pattern of "Clap Your Hands" as a mystery song. Let the children guess the name of the song.

3. Sing the song and clap the beat while you point to the beats on the chart, moving from line to line without losing the beat.
4. Choose a child to keep the beat on the chart while the class sings the song.
5. Tell the children that the symbols on the chart are called "ta's" and they will use this rhythm syllable everytime they read

| | | |
ta ta ta ta

6. Read the chart with ta's and clap the beat.

OTHER SONGS TO USE

"Marching to Praetoria" • "Row, Row, Row Your Boat" • "Yankee Doodle."

There are inumerable songs that can be used with this chart, but until the children are confident with the beat, it would be wise to avoid songs that have an **anacrusis** or pick-up. (These are songs that *do not* begin on the first beat.)

ADDITIONAL ACTIVITIES

1. Select a song appropriate to the grade level. Use the song as a mystery song by clapping the pattern. The child who correctly identifies the song can be the "teacher" and keep the beat on the chart while the class sings the song.
2. Choose a familiar song to sing and decide which instrument would be appropriate as an accompaniment. For example,

   "Twinkle, Twinkle"—triangle, finger
   cymbals
   "Yankee Doodle"—drum, sticks
   "Row, Row, Row Your Boat"—sand
   blocks

3. To encourage musical discrimination, let the children decide which instrument to use.
4. Encourage the children to decide whether the instrumental accompaniment should be loud or soft.

EVALUATION OF RHYTHMIC AND PERCEPTUAL SKILLS

Psychomotor Development and Perception

1. Can the children walk the beat with increasing confidence?
2. Can the children turn the phrases without losing the beat (position in space)?

Aural and Visual Acuity and Perception

1. Can the children follow the beats on the chart with their eyes moving from left to right and from line to line?
2. Can the children identify a mystery song?

Musical Development and Social Maturity

1. Can the children choose an appropriate instrument for a song?
2. Can the children decide whether the song should be loud or soft, either with their voices or playing an instrument?
3. Do the children contribute to the song by creating new verses? Suggesting and playing an instrument? Singing with enjoyment? Accepting the ideas of others?

Inner Hearing

Kentucky Singing Game

1. Where, oh, where is pret-ty lit-tle Nel - lie?

Where, oh, where is pret-ty lit-tle Nel - lie?

Where, oh, where is pret-ty lit-tle Nel - lie?

Way down yon-der in the paw paw patch.

2. Come on, boys, and let's go find her. (3 times)
Way down yonder in the paw paw patch.

3. Pickin' up' paw paw, puttin' in a basket (3 times)
Way down yonder in the paw paw patch.

PREPARATION FOR THE CHART

1. Teach the song. There are many variations to this song. Change the name to someone in your class.
2. Sing the song and clap the beat.
3. Sing the song and step the beat.
4. Sing the song and clap the pattern (words).
5. Sing the song and put the pattern in the feet.
6. Sing the song, clap the pattern, and walk the beat.
7. For more mature children, sing the song, clap the pattern, walk the beat, and turn the phrases.
8. Sing the song, clap "Where, oh, where is" and step "pretty little Nellie." Clap and step "Way down yonder in the paw paw patch."

INTRODUCE THE CHART

1. Discuss the illustrations. What do they mean?
2. Point to the beats on Line 1. Say the ta's.
3. Point to the beats on Line 2. Step the ta's
4. Explain to the class that the heart means to put the beat inside, and it is therefore silent. Point to the beats on Line 3. Feel the beat.

[Note: From now on, this will be referred to as **inner hearing,** which is an important part of musical training.]

5. Point to the beats on Line 4. Clap the ta's.
6. Clap "Paw Paw Patch" as a mystery song.
7. Sing the song while the teacher points to the beats on the chart.
8. Repeat the song or sing the next verse and follow the directions on the chart: sing Line 1, step Line 2, feel Line 3, and clap Line 4.
9. Vary the order of the chart by starting on Line 2 or Line 3.
10. Have one child keep the beats on the chart while the class sings the song. He may start on any line he wishes.

14

OTHER SONGS TO USE

"Are You Sleeping • "Down By the Station" • "Looby Loo."

This chart can be used with numerous songs and should be used often during the year. However, until the children have had many experiences and feel confident with the beat, avoid songs that have an anacrusis or pick-up.

ADDITIONAL ACTIVITIES

1. Make flash cards of the illustrations on the chart:

Select a familiar song to sing and change the cards at random while the children are singing. This activity can be expanded to include flash cards of rhythm instruments playing the beat and later the pattern. When the instrument is playing, the rest of the class is silent.

2. *Radio Game:* Through the inquiry method, let the children decide which motion is used to turn "on" a radio. When the radio is turned "off," does the music stop at the radio station? The children will soon decide that the music continues, even though their set is turned off.

Select a song. Turn the radio "on" (imaginary knob) and start singing the song. Turn the radio "off" but keep the song going inside. Turn the radio back "on". Did everyone come in on the same word? Play this game, turning the radio "on" or "off" at random, not necessarily by phrase. Choose different children to operate the radio.

EVALUATION OF RHYTHMIC AND PERCEPTUAL SKILLS

Psychomotor Development and Perception

1. Can the children move from one activity to another without losing the beat?
2. Can the children play a rhythm instrument while reading the chart?

Aural Acuity and Perception

1. Can the children feel the beat inside them?
2. Can they sing the song inside them and not lose the beat or the melody?

Visual Acuity and Perception

1. Can the children read the symbols and go from line to line without losing the beat?
2. Can their eyes follow the rhythm symbols on the chart, moving from left to right and from line to line?

Musical Development and Social Maturity

1. Are the children becoming increasingly aware of the beat of a song?
2. Are the children becoming increasingly aware of the phrases within a song? Can they demonstrate this with body movements?

Phrasing

Traditional

Yank - ee Doo - dle went to town a - rid - ing on a po — ny,

Stuck a feath - er in his cap and called it mac - a - ro — ni.

Refrain

Yank - ee Doo - dle, keep it up, Yank - ee Doo - dle dan — dy,

Mind the mu - sic and the step, And with the girls be han - dy.

Phrasing

PREPARATION FOR THE CHART

1. Teach the song.
2. Sing the song and clap the beat.
3. Sing the song and step or walk the beat.
4. Sing the song and clap the pattern.
5. Sing the song and step the pattern.
6. Sing the song, step the pattern and clap the beat.

INTRODUCE THE CHART

1. Ask the children what the song says first.

   "Yankee Doodle went to town
   a-riding on a pony"

   This is the first phrase.
2. Point to the chart and sing the first phrase, using either illustrations or beats.

3. Point to the chart and sing the second phrase.
4. Point to the beats, saying and clapping the ta's (I).
5. Point to the beats on the chart, sing the song, and make large arm movements for each phrase—first with the right arm, then with the left arm.

   [Note: Tell the children they are making the motion for a "phrase." Add this word to their musical vocabulary.]

6. Choose a child to keep the beat on the chart while the class sings the song. Be sure to keep the beat while going from phrase to phrase.
7. Sing the song and tap the ta's on the chart—the first phrase with the fingers of

the right hand, the second phrase with the knuckles of the left hand. Repeat for phrases three and four.

8. Point to the beats on the chart, sing "Yankee Doodle" then put the song inside (inner hearing), follow the beats through the song, and all sing "macaroni" together. Repeat this activity for phrases three and four.

9. The last activity can be varied by singing the first and last word of each phrase and clapping or stepping the beat for inner hearing.

OTHER SONGS TO USE

"Three Pirates" • "Old Woman" • "Are You Sleeping."

[Note: Let the children decide where the phrases occur. Some songs may have four beats to a phrase and some may have eight or more beats to a phrase. Encourage the children to decide whether the phrases are identical or different (A–B, A–B–A, A–A–B, etc.). This is the beginning of understanding **form** *in music.]*

ADDITIONAL ACTIVITIES

1. Choose a familiar song to sing and decide where the phrases occur. While singing the song, make the phrase marks on a large piece of paper.

[Note: The tendency of children when beginning this activity is to make the first phrase from left to right and the second phrase from right to left:

This is acceptable but does not follow the pattern of musical notation or the printed page. Encourage the children to make the phrase markings from left to right:

Some songs will have more than two phrases. Let the children discover this and decide how many phrases there should be.]

2. Select a song to sing and, while singing, make the beat marks on a large piece of paper or on the chalkboard. The beats (I) should be by phrase in 4 or 8:

"Are you sleeping? Are you sleeping?"
  I I I I   I I I I

"Swing, Swing, Swing, Swing"
  I   I   I   I

EVALUATION OF RHYTHMIC AND PERCEPTUAL SKILLS

Psychomotor Development and Perception

1. Can the children change direction and keep the beat (position in space)?
2. Can they change from a gross motor activity to a fine motor activity?

   • walking the beat for one phrase.
   • tapping the beat for the next phrase.

Aural and Visual Acuity and Perception

1. Can the children sing the song and feel the phrase?
2. Can the children match the beats on the chart to the song?

Musical Development and Social Maturity

1. Do the children have an increasing awareness of musical form?

   • identical phrases: A–A
   • phrases that are different: A–B
   • repetition: A–B–A

2. Is there an increasing spontaneity while singing a song?
3. Do the children volunteer to be the "teacher" (leadership)?
4. Do they listen to others? Follow directions?

5

The Rest

The Rest

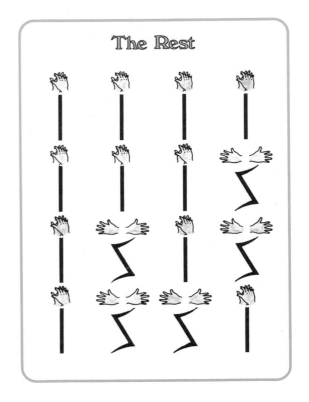

The Rest

The **rest** (𝄽) is silent but has a beat. Clap the beats (I—ta) and throw the rest away:

The rest is the rhythm symbol for silence, but the beat continues.

INTRODUCE THE CHART

1. Select one child to read and clap the first line of the chart.
2. What do they see at the end of the second line? Tell the children that this is the symbol or sign for a rest. The beat is silent and they make the rest motion by throwing their hands out and say "rest" or "sh." (The sound "sh" is known around the world for silence.) For more mature children, make the rest motion and feel the silence (silent beat).
3. Choose individual children to read one line of the chart while you point to the beats on the chart.
4. Read and clap the entire chart without losing the beat, saying the ta's and "sh" or "rest" for the rest.
5. Sing "Twinkle, Twinkle" and clap and read the first two lines of the chart.

[*Note: These two lines are repeated six times for the complete song.*]

6. Choose a child to point to the rhythm symbols on the chart while the class sings "Twinkle, Twinkle," being careful to keep the beat throughout the song:

Twin-kle, Twin-kle | Lit-tle Star
I   I   I   I | I   I   I   𝄽

7. Sing "Marching to Praetoria" while reading and clapping Line 3 of the chart:

I 𝄽 I 𝄽

8. Sing "Are You Sleeping" and read and clap Line 4 of the chart through the entire song. Point to the rhythm symbols on the chart while the class sings the song:

I 𝄽 𝄽 I

9. Select a familiar song, step the beat, and read and clap the entire chart, moving from line to line without losing the beat. The chart will probably have to be repeated several times for the complete song. Choose a child to act as the leader by keeping the beat and pointing to the rhythm symbols on the chart.

OTHER SONGS TO USE

This chart can be used in many different ways, depending on the maturity of your class. Sing the song and clap one line or the entire chart.

"Shoo Fly" • "Old Brass Wagon" • "Skip To My Lou."

ADDITIONAL ACTIVITIES

1. Clap variations and children echo with ta's and clapping, making the motion for the rest (echo clapping):

Teacher claps	Children say and clap (on the beat)
I I I ₹	ta–ta–ta–sh (or rest)
I ₹ I ₹	ta–sh–ta–sh
I ₹ ₹ I	ta–sh–sh–ta
₹ ₹ I I	sh–sh–ta–ta

2. *Dictation:* Have class write down patterns after they say and clap them.

[Note: The rest is made by slanting the ta (\\), then adding an arm (⌐) and a leg (⌐). Have the children practice making the rest on the chalkboard and on tracing paper to give them confidence.]

Teacher claps	Class says and claps	Class writes
I I I ₹	ta–ta–ta–sh	I I I ₹
I ₹ I ₹	ta–sh–ta–sh	I ₹ I ₹
₹ ₹ ₹ I	sh–sh–sh–ta	₹ ₹ ₹ I

3. Make flash cards of various patterns:

Show one card. Class responds by clapping and ta's. Try to keep the beat while going from card to card.

4. Select four children to dramatize the pattern:

Teacher claps   Children dramatize

Use variations of the pattern.

5. *Mirror Image and Echo Clapping:* Clap pattern variations on different parts of the body or on objects in the room. For example, head–knees, stomach–table, nose–floor, right side–left side, etc. Move from pattern to pattern without losing the beat.

6. Choose a familiar song. Decide on a pattern to clap throughout the entire song. Write the pattern on the chalkboard.

7. Sing a familiar song. Have one group of children play a pattern (I ₹ I I) on rhythm instruments to accompany the song. This pattern is an **ostinato.**

[Note: Tell the children the word "ostinato" is Italian and means "stubborn," so they must hold on to the pattern. Add this word to their musical vocabulary.]

8. Select a child to lead the class in echo clapping and mirror image, using variations of a pattern. When the leader loses the beat, he sits down and another child becomes the leader.

EVALUATION OF RHYTHMIC AND PERCEPTUAL SKILLS

Aural Acuity and Perception

Can the children recognize and read the rest as a silent beat?

Psychomotor Development and Perception

1. Can the children step a pattern containing rests (position in space)?
2. Can the children sing a song and play a given pattern on a rhythm instrument?
3. Can the children echo a given pattern on various parts of the body?
4. Do they have a growing awareness of right and left?

Old MacDonald

PREPARATION FOR THE CHART

1. Teach the song.
2. Sing the song and let the class decide which animal to sing next. What kind of a sound does the animal make?
3. Choose one child to sing "And on his farm he had a _____." Continue with each verse sung by a different child.

INTRODUCE THE CHART

1. Read the pattern with clapping and ta's. Make the rest motion.

   [*Note: When reading the pattern to a specific song, it is not necessary to make the "sh" sound for the rest. This is only when reading a rhythm pattern or when the class is insecure.*]

2. Point to the pattern on the chart and sing the song, keeping the beat.

3. Select one child to be the leader and point to the chart while the class sings the song. Each leader will choose the next animal to add to the song.
4. Point to the pattern on the chart, sing the song, and dramatize each animal with gross arm movements.

ADDITIONAL ACTIVITIES

1. Sing the song without the chart and have the children write the pattern on the chalkboard or a large piece of paper (verse only).
2. Sing the song, walk the beat, and turn each phrase of the verse. Continue walking the beat for the refrain but dramatize each animal, either by style of walking (waddle—duck) or arm motions (wiggle ears—mule).
3. Sing the song, but clap the pattern on the animal sounds. (This is an activity for the more mature children.)
4. Sing the song and have one group of children play a pattern on rhythm instruments (ostinato).
5. Sing the song sitting on the floor or on a chair:

   > First beat—slap knees
   > Second beat—clap
   > Third beat—slap knees
   > Fourth beat—clap

   Continue this activity through the entire song.
6. Use variations of the above activity.

   - Sit facing a partner. First beat clap hands, second beat clap partners hands, etc.
   - Sit in a circle close enough to touch the persons hands on either side with outstretched arms. Clap own hands on first beat and then clap the hands of

the two people on either side, etc. (peripheral vision). Be sure to keep the beat while singing the song.
7. Assign a rhythm instrument for each animal and distribute to individual children. Sing the song and when a specific animal is sung, the child must play his instrument on the beat (e.g., oink, oink—sticks).

EVALUATION OF RHYTHMIC AND PERCEPTUAL SKILLS

Visual Acuity and Perception

1. Can the children's eyes follow the pattern on the chart from line to line?
2. Can the children clap hands with adjacent partners, using peripheral vision, without losing the beat.

OLD MACDONALD

Traditional

OldMac-Don-ald had a farm, Ee - i - ee - i - oh. And on his farm he had a pig,

Ee - i - ee - i - oh. With an oink, oink here, and an oink, oink there, Here an oink,

there an oink, Eve - rywhere an oink, oink. OldMac-Don-aldhad a farm, Ee - i - ee - i - oh.

1. Old MacDonald had a farm,
   Ee-i-ee-i-oh,
   And on his farm he had a pig,
   Ee-i-ee-i-oh.

   Refrain:

   With an oink, oink here,
   And an oink, oink, there,
   Here an oink, there an oink,
   Everywhere an oink, oink.

2. Old MacDonald had a farm,
   Ee-i-ee-i-oh,
   And on his farm he had a duck,
   Ee-i-ee-i-oh.

   Refrain:

   With a quack, quack here,
   And a quack, quack there,
   Here a quack, there a quack,
   Everywhere a quack, quack.
   Oink, oink here,
   And an oink, oink there,
   etc.

[*Note: This is a cumulative song. Let the children add an animal for each verse and decide what kind of sound the animal makes.*]

I Can Play

The use of instruments involves a more integrated set of motions combining singing, reading the symbols on the chart, and fine motor skills. This involvement will have a direct relationship to learning activities in other areas of the curriculum. Use this chart many times with familiar songs and favorite recordings. Encourage the children to use musical discrimination and to become aware of loud and soft. For example,

> drum—loud: "Yankee Doodle"
> triangle—soft: "Twinkle, Twinkle"
> sticks—medium loud: "Down by
> the Station"

If you feel that your class is ready to expand their musical vocabulary, introduce these musical terms:

p—*piano:* soft (*piano* means soft in Italian)
pp—*pianissimo:* very soft
f—*forte:* loud (*forte* means loud in Italian)
mf—*mezzo-forte:* medium-loud (*mezzo* means half or middle in Italian)
ff—*fortissimo:* very loud

PREPARATION FOR THE CHART

1. Introduce the rhythm instruments shown on the chart.
2. Clap the pattern of a familiar song without singing. Let the children guess the name of the song **(mystery song)**. Sing the song and clap the pattern.
3. Ask the children which instrument would sound best as an accompaniment to the song. Should the song be sung softly or vigorously (loud does not mean to shout)? Some examples are:

"Are You Sleeping?": triangle—*piano* (soft)
"Sandy Land": sand blocks—*mezzo-forte* (medium-loud)
"Yankee Doodle": drum—*forte* (loud)

INTRODUCE THE CHART

1. Point to the first line of the chart. What sound does the drum make (boom)? Is the drum playing the last beat? Dramatize playing the drum on Line 1, say "boom" and make the sign for the rest. Is a drum loud or soft?
2. Point to the second line of the chart. What sound does the triangle make (ting)? Where do the rests occur (second and fourth beat)? Dramatize playing the triangle on Line 2, say "ting" and make the signs for the rests. Is a triangle loud or soft?
3. Point to Line 3 of the chart. Select one child to read the chart and dramatize playing the sticks. What sound do the sticks make (click)? Let the class echo with imaginary sticks.
4. Read the illustrations on the chart without losing the beat. Dramatize playing and make the sound of the instrument as you read the chart.

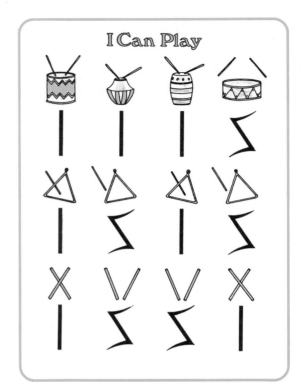

I Can Play

[*Note: Encourage the children to change their voices to fit the instrument, from the deep sound of the drum to the high, thin sound of the triangle, and the sharp sound of the sticks.*]

5. Choose one child to be the leader and point to the rhythm symbols (I, 𝄽) on the chart while the class claps and says the rhythm syllables (ta or rest).
6. Select a familiar song and clap one line of the chart as an ostinato (Chart 5) while one child keeps the beat on the chart. As the children become more confident, clap the entire chart as an accompaniment.)

Drum

"Marching to Praetoria" • "In Bahia" • "Land of the Silver Birch."

Triangle

"Hush, Little Baby" • "Are You Sleeping?" • "Little Ducklings."

Sticks

"Who's That Knocking at My Window?" • "Over the River" (two beats to a measure) • "Down by the Station."

ADDITIONAL ACTIVITIES

1. Make a large classroom chart with drawings or pictures of the instruments available in the classroom. Let the children decide what words describe the sound each instrument makes. Put the pictures on the left of the chart and their sound on the right:

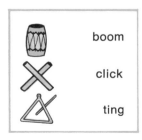

Select a song and divide the class. Have one group sing the song while the other group dramatizes playing and sounding the instrument that you point to on the chart. Skip from one illustration to another without losing the beat.

2. Select a song, divide the class into several groups. Pass out various instruments pictured on the chart. Choose a leader to point to this chart while the class sings the song. The leader may change the instrument whenever he chooses and the class must be ready to play only when it is their turn.

3. Make flash cards of various patterns using ta's and rests:

As you show each card, those children having the instrument on the card must play the pattern. When the class becomes more confident, you can use the cards as an instrumental accompaniment to a song.

EVALUATION OF RHYTHMIC AND PERCEPTUAL SKILLS

Aural and Visual Acuity and Perception

1. Do the children show increasing awareness of the appropriate sounds to accompany a song?
2. Do the children look at the charts or flash cards and read the correct pattern and play the instrument pictured?

Bingo

1. Teach the song.
2. Sing the song and clap the beat. To make the motion for the anacrusis, extend both arms to the side, and clap the first beat:

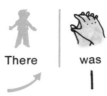

There | was

3. Sing the song and clap the pattern, using the motion for the anacrusis and accent the first beat.
4. Sing the song and play the traditional game. Clap the "B" instead of singing, then "B–I," and continue until all the letters are clapped.)
5. Sing the song and step the beat while clapping the pattern.
6. Step the pattern while singing the song.
7. All sing "There," and then put the song inside, feeling the beat; all sing the last word "name-O" together (inner hearing).
8. Choose a child to clap the pattern of the song as a mystery song.

INTRODUCE THE CHART

1. Tell the children they must "Bark" and clap every time the dog is in his house and be silent and make the rest motion when there is no dog.
2. Choose one child to point to the rhythm symbols on the chart while the class reads and claps the ta's and rests.
3. Ask the children what the "arrow" means on the chart (anacrusis or pick-up).
4. Sing the song "Bingo," using the motion for the anacrusis and clap the chart while singing the song.

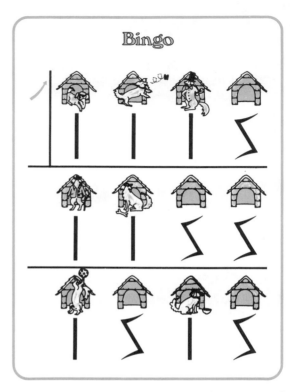

[Note: The chart will have to be repeated to sing the whole song. Move from the bottom of the chart to the first ta at the top without losing the beat.]

5. Divide the class. One group will sing "Bingo" while the other group "barks" the pattern. Have one child point to the chart.

[Note: Be sure to allow for the anacrusis before the first group begins to "bark."]

6. Repeat the last activity several times and then combine the two groups without pointing to the chart. Let the leader give the motion for the anacrusis ("There") and lead both groups by keeping the beat (just like a conductor), moving his hands up and down. Later the class will learn the conducting pattern for 2/4.

*[Note: Many of the songs that children sing have an **anacrusis** or pick-up. This simply means that a song does not start on the first beat of the measure but on the up-beat or a portion of the preceding measure. This will naturally put the accent on the following measure. Several familiar examples are given below:]*

Oh | <u>say</u> can you | see . . .

Mine | <u>eyes</u> have seen the glory . . .

She'll be | <u>comin'</u> 'round the mountain . . . .

Introduce the word "anacrusis" to the children. They will enjoy using it and it will become part of their musical vocabulary.]

BINGO

Scottish Folksong

There was a farm-er had a dog and Bing-o was his name - O,

B - I - N - G - O, B - I - N - G - O, B - I - N - G - O and Bing-o was his name-O!

OTHER SONGS TO USE

Using only the rhythm symbols, this chart can be used with the following songs.

"Band of Angels"   There was | <u>one</u> . . .

"If You're Happy"   If you're | <u>happy</u> . . .

"Billy Boy"   Oh | <u>where</u> . . .

ADDITIONAL ACTIVITIES

1. Teach the song "Oh, Where Has My Little Dog Gone?" Clap the beat while singing the song, using the motion for the ana-crusis ("Oh, <u>where</u> . . .").

   [Note: The beat for this song is in 3 rather than the familiar 4 or 2.]

   Sing the song and clap the rhythm symbols on the chart *vertically.* Sing the song and "bark" the chart vertically. Sing the song and play the chart on rhythm instruments.

2. Clap the chart with different songs, reading it horizontally for songs that have 2 or 4 beats and vertically for songs that have 3 beats.

3. When using the chart vertically, step the beat with the accent on the first beat and tiptoe the second and third beats (preparation for the waltz).

   step   tip–toe,   step   tip–toe
   <u>1</u>   2   3   <u>1</u>   2   3

EVALUATION OF RHYTHMIC AND PERCEPTUAL SKILLS

Psychomotor Development and Perception

1. Can the children, through motor activities, feel the accent of the song?
2. Can the children read the chart and play an instrument?
3. Are the children becoming increasingly confident while performing integrated activities?

Aural Acuity and Perception

1. Are the children becoming increasingly confident with rhythm patterns using the silent beat (rest)?
2. Can they recognize different meters (three and four)?

Visual Acuity and Perception

Can the children read a chart and clap the pattern, using ta's and rests?

Rhythms

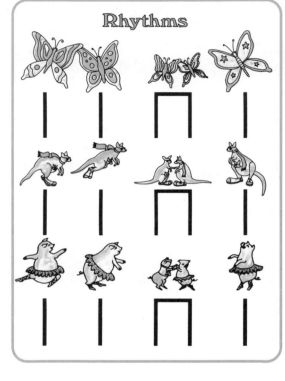

[Note: Charts 9, 10, and 11 teach the same basic concept, and therefore the "Evaluation of Rhythmic and Perceptual Skills" for these charts appears at the end of Chart 11.]

PREPARATION FOR THE CHART

[Note: In the preceding charts, the rhythm pattern was a combination of beats and rests (❘, 𝄾). Now, we have a new symbol (⊓, ti), which has two sounds to the beat (ti–ti), but has the same duration as ta (❘). Ta (❘) is a quarter note (♩) and ti–ti (⊓) is two eighth notes (♫).]

Ask the children to clap the pattern of their name (syllabication).

Kath–leen Fla–her–ty: ❘ ❘ ⊓ ❘
John Brown: ❘ 𝄾 ❘ 𝄾 or ♩ ♩
Mar–y Ann Bergovich: ⊓ ❘ ⊓ ❘

INTRODUCE THE CHART

1. Point to the illustrations on the chart and clap the pattern of the words:

    Line 1:   Fly, fly, butter–fly
    Line 2:   Roo, roo, kanga–roo
    Line 3:   Pig, pig, little pig

   Encourage the children to use their voices to describe the illustrations. (Would a "butterfly" sound like a "kangaroo?")

2. Point to the illustrations on the chart and say and step the pattern of the words. Do you step the same way for the kangaroo and the little pig?

3. Point to the rhythm pattern on the chart. Is there something new? Tell the class whenever they see ⊓ they will read "ti–ti."

4. Point to the rhythm symbols and read and clap the entire chart with ta's and ti's. (Do not point to each small figure, only the first one of the pair, for that is where you feel the beat.)

5. Select individual children to read and clap the rhythm symbols of one line of the chart while you keep the beat.

6. Select a leader to keep the beat while the class reads and claps the entire chart with ta's and ti's.

7. Proceed to the next chart.

10

More Rhythms

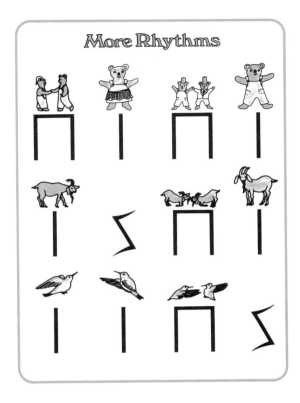
INTRODUCE THE CHART

1. Clap the pattern of each of the illustrations (syllabication).

> Ted–dy bear
> Bil–ly goat
> Hum–ming bird

2. Clap the pattern of each line of the chart, using words rather than rhythm syllables:

> Ted–dy bear, Ted–dy bear
> Goat ≀ Bil–ly goat
> Bird, bird, hum–ming ≀

3. Read and clap the entire chart without losing the beat.

4. Read and clap the entire chart, using rhythm syllables (ta and ti).

5. Select a leader to keep the beat on the chart while the class reads and claps the rhythm syllables.

6. Divide the class into three groups. Assign one line of the chart to each group. Clap the rhythm symbols and dramatize the animal, moving from one line to the next without losing the beat.

[*Note: As the children become more confident and proficient, they will be able to do the above activity without a leader. This involves feeling the beat inside and using visual perception to interpret the symbols on the chart.*]

OTHER SONGS TO USE

Using Charts 7 through 10, clap or play a rhythmic accompaniment or ostinato to familiar songs. Encourage the children to use musical discrimination for appropriate sounds.

''Sandy Land''—sand blocks • ''Battle Hymn of the Republic'' (refrain)—drum • ''Bow, Belinda''—sticks.

ADDITIONAL ACTIVITIES

1. Starting with Chart 7, move from chart to chart without losing the beat, using previous rhythmic experiences:

- clapping
- stepping
- inner hearing
- tapping

2. Clap the pattern, the class echoes the clapped pattern and then echoes the rhythm syllables (ta, ta, ti–ti, ta). Use various patterns of ta's, ti's, and rests:

Leader claps	Children clap	Children say
⏐ ⊓ ⏐ ⏐	⏐ ⊓ ⏐ ⏐	ta ti–ti ta ta
⊓ ⏐ ⊓ ⏐	⊓ ⏐ ⊓ ⏐	ti–ti ta ti–ti ta
⏐ ≀ ⊓ ⏐	⏐ ≀ ⊓ ⏐	ta rest ti–ti ta

The patterns can be as difficult as the children are capable of doing.

3. Proceed to the next chart.

Mystery Songs

INTRODUCE THE CHART

1. This chart can be used as a game. Clap one of the rhythm patterns on the chart, and have the children identify which one was clapped by raising one finger for Line 1, two fingers for Line 2, and three fingers for Line 3.
2. Clap one of the rhythm patterns on the chart. The child who correctly identifies the song may lead the class while they sing the song (mystery song). If the child is confident, he may wish to sing the song by himself.
3. Choose one child to keep the beat on the chart while the class claps the patterns and reads the ta's and ti's, moving from line to line without losing the beat.
4. Select a familiar song to sing and use one line on the chart as a rhythmic ostinato with clapping or stepping.
5. For the more advanced children, try using all three lines of the chart as an ostinato. Start the first ostinato to establish the beat, then add the second ostinato, and finally the third. Begin to sing the song. (As the children become more confident, all parts can begin together.) For example,

Song: "Are You Sleeping?"
First instrument: triangle—l l ⊓ l
Second instrument: sticks or
   chopsticks—⊓ ⊓ l l
Third instrument: jingle
   stick—l ⊓ l l
Class sings the song.

OTHER SONGS TO USE

"Four in the Boat"—ta ti–ti ta ti–ti
                              (l   ⊓   l   ⊓)
"Old Woman"—ta ti–ti ta ti–ti (l ⊓ l ⊓)
"Skip to My Lou"—ta ti–ti ti–ti ta (l ⊓ ⊓ l)

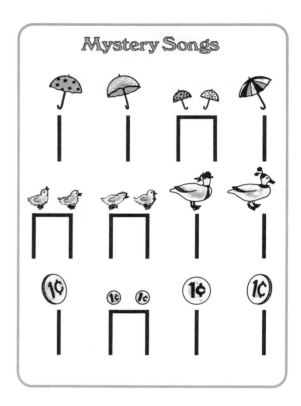

Mystery Songs

ADDITIONAL ACTIVITIES

1. *Echo Clapping and Dictation*

Teacher claps	Class echo claps and says syllables	Class writes
l ⊓ l ⁊	ta ti–ti ta rest	l ⊓ l ⁊
⊓ l ⊓ ⊓	ti–ti ta ti–ti ti–ti	⊓ l ⊓ ⊓
l ⁊ ⊓ ⁊	ta rest ti–ti rest	l ⁊ ⊓ ⁊

[Note: Be sure to make the motion for the rest when clapping the rhythm pattern.]

PREPARATION FOR THE CHART

[Note: This chart is a continuation of the preceding two charts and is based on previous learnings. The use of various combinations of rhythm symbols will provide a greater variety of rhythmic experiences and contribute to the child's confidence in the psychomotor domain.]

1. Teach the songs.
2. Sing the songs and use previous rhythmic experiences:

   • Clap the beat • Clap the pattern • Step the beat and clap the pattern • Combine these activities • Walk the beat and turn the phrase • Use the rhythm patterns as a mystery song • inner hearing.

RAIN, RAIN GO AWAY

Traditional

Rain, rain go a - way, Come a - gain an - o - ther day.

LITTLE DUCKLINGS

German Folk Song

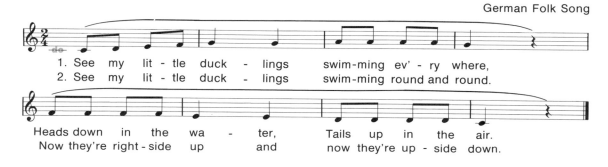

1. See my lit - tle duck - lings swim-ming ev' - ry where,
2. See my lit - tle duck - lings swim-ming round and round.

Heads down in the wa - ter, Tails up in the air.
Now they're right - side up and now they're up - side down.

WHO HAS THE PENNY

Traditional Game Song

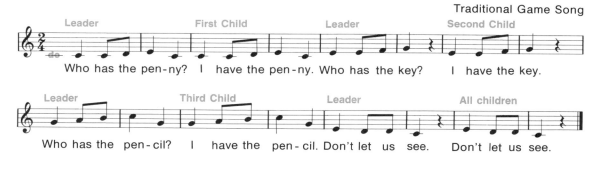

Leader · First Child · Leader · Second Child

Who has the pen - ny? I have the pen - ny. Who has the key? I have the key.

Leader · Third Child · Leader · All children

Who has the pen - cil? I have the pen - cil. Don't let us see. Don't let us see.

2. *Echo Clapping with Mirror Image.* Remember to keep the beat when moving from one rhythm pattern to another.

Teacher claps				Class echoes			
hands	I	I	⊓ I	hands	I	I	⊓ I
knees	⊓	I	⊓ I	knees	⊓	I	⊓ I
floor	⊓	⊓	I I	floor	⊓	⊓	I I

[*Note: Try to have a different tone quality for each rhythm pattern.*]

3. Make flash cards of different rhythm patterns. At first, use the flash cards with the class and later with individuals.
4. Dramatize a rhythm pattern. Choose four children to represent the beat, and clap

a rhythm pattern. The class echoes with clapping and ta's and ti's. The four children who are chosen to represent the beats must decide whether any beat has two sounds. If a beat has two sounds the child representing that beat must select someone in the class to be the second sound. For example, I I ⊓ I might be:

EVALUATION OF RHYTHMIC AND PERCEPTUAL SKILLS

Psychomotor Development and Perception

Are the children developing the ability to coordinate more than one activity, using diverse patterns?

- clapping a pattern—stepping a beat
- eye-hand coordination
- reading a chart—playing an instrument

Aural Acuity and Perception

1. Can the children hear of the silent beat (𝄽)?
2. Can the children hear long and short sounds (I, ⊓)?
3. Can the children identify familiar patterns (mystery songs)?

Visual Acuity and Perception

1. Are the children becoming increasingly confident while reading rhythm symbols on the chart?
2. Can the children identify long and short sounds visually?
3. Can their eyes follow the pattern on the chart, moving from line to line and chart to chart without losing the beat?

Jump Rope

PREPARATION FOR THE CHART

Jump-rope chants are found around the world and each geographical area has its favorite. In some neighborhoods, children say "Delawarey" instead of "Delaware" for this jump–rope chant. If this variation occurs, use it as a learning situation and let the children decide how the rhythm pattern should be altered (Line 2—⊓ ⊓ | ⟨).

[Note: Regional differences of all chants or songs should be employed as a teaching aid to enhance the further learning of rhythm patterns and syllabication.]

INTRODUCE THE CHART

1. Read the jump rope chant with the children.
2. Read the chart again and clap the words (pattern).

3. Clap and read the rhythm syllables on the chart (ta's–ti's).
4. Read and clap the rhythm syllables and step or jump the beat.
5. Step the rhythm pattern and clap the beat while reading the chant.

[Note: This is a highly integrated activity and might pose some problems at first. The children are usually more successful than the teacher.]

6. Chant and clap the first phrase of the chart:

Ice cream soda, Delaware punch,
Chant and step the second phrase.

Tell me the name of your Honeybunch.

OTHER CHANTS TO USE

"Teddy Bear"

Teddy bear, Teddy bear,
Turn around.
Teddy bear, Teddy bear,
Touch the ground.
Teddy bear, Teddy bear,
Show your shoe.
Teddy Bear, Teddy bear,
That will do.

"Over the Ocean"

Over the ocean, Over the sea.
Johnny broke a bottle and
    blamed it on me.
I told Ma, She told Pa.
Johnny got a lickin' so
Ha! Ha! Ha!

Ice cream soda.
Delaware punch.
Tell me the name of your
Honeybunch.

ADDITIONAL ACTIVITIES

1. "Over the Ocean" is a good chant for encouraging children to create their own charts with rhythm symbols and illustrations. Start with dictation, line by line.

Teacher says	Children clap and say syllables
Over the ocean,	ta ti–ti ta ta
Over the sea,	ta ti–ti ta rest
Johnny broke a	ti–ti ti–ti
bottle and . . .	ti–ti ta

Have children write rhythm symbols on a piece of paper.

2. *Roll Call*

Teacher calls name	Child answers with rhythm syllables
Mary Jones	ti–ti ta
Michael Connaly	ta ta ti–ti ta
Gary Medford	ta ta ta ta

3. *Tapping.* Tap a pattern; have the class answer with ta's and ti's, while writing the pattern on paper or the chalkboard.
4. *Poetry.* Write the poem or words to a song on the board and read it to the class. Read the poem aloud together; then write the pattern. Be sure the words have a definite pattern and rhythm and are within the ability of your class. Some good ones to use are "Taffy," "Are You Sleeping?" and "Ten Little Indians."
5. Use a jump rope to keep the beat. Chant a jump rope chant while one child jumps rope. When the child loses the beat (misses), another child gets a turn.

[Note: Some children can jump rope faster than others and the chant should be adapted to the ability of the "jumper." The children will then have an introduction to **tempo** (fast and slow). The object is to keep the beat and not miss.]

EVALUATION OF RHYTHMIC AND PERCEPTUAL SKILLS

Psychomotor Development and Perception

Are the children becoming more confident while performing echo clapping? • writing a pattern? • balance and coordination activities? • gross motor activities?

Aural and Visual Acuity and Perception

1. Can the children write a familiar poem or words to a song in rhythm symbols? (syllabication)?
2. Can the children recognize a rhythm pattern and relate the pattern to a familiar song or poem?

Ostinato

[Note: This chart is a speaking-rhythm chart in two parts. The symbols are the same. The variety in a spoken rhythm is introduced by the manner in which the voice is used, providing tone color. The "Evaluation of Rhythmic and Perceptual Skills" is combined with that of Chart 14.]

PREPARATION FOR THE CHART

1. Create verbal story pictures and let the children decide how they would say the following:

   Fire! Fire!—Loudly, with intensity (ff)
   Go to sleep—Softly, tenderly (pp)
   Here kitty, kitty, kitty—gently (mp)

2. Would they use a loud voice or a soft voice? Would they be excited or calm?

INTRODUCE THE CHART

1. Ask individual children to read and clap the rhythm symbols of each line of the chart.

2. Is there something new on the chart (repeat signs: ‖: :‖)?

3. Tell the children that the double bar with two dots is a repeat sign. Everytime they see this sign it means they must repeat what they have just sung or played, either from the beginning of the song or back to the first repeat sign (‖:).

4. What is the word over the third line of the chart (ostinato)? Many children will be able to sound out the word. Do they remember what it means?

5. How would the children use their voices to say "Keep cool" (calm and low—mp)?

6. How would they use their voices to say "Simmer down" (a little louder with their voices sharply accented—mf)?

7. How would the children say "worry, worry, worry, worry"? This chart can be developed into a dramatic story of a disagreement on the playground and the final apprehension at being "caught" for misbehaving (worry, worry).

8. Divide the class into two groups. Group 1 says "Keep cool" and "Simmer down" with repeats, changing their voices to provide contrast. Those in Group 2 are the "worriers" (ostinato).

[Note: When introducing this activity, establish the beat with the ostinato (Group 2), then Group 1 enters with "Keep cool" and "Simmer down." When the children become more confident, Group 1 and Group 2 can begin at the same time. Establish the beat before the class begins to read the chart.]

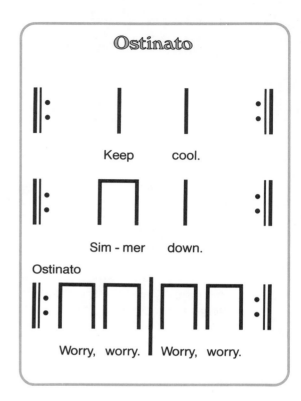

OTHER MATERIAL TO USE

Create original rhythm patterns from the children's language experiences, such as original stories, reading, and individual experiences. Here are some examples:

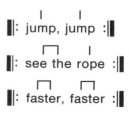

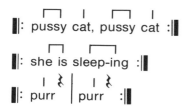

‖: pussy cat, pussy cat :‖

‖: she is sleep-ing :‖

‖: purr | purr :‖

The ostinato can be decided by the teacher or leader. Let the children decide whether their voices should be loud or soft, calm or excited, etc.

ADDITIONAL ACTIVITIES

1. Divide the class into two groups and read the chart with sound differentiation:

   Group 1:   rapping the desk
   Group 2:   clapping

   Group 1:   rhythm sticks
   Group 2:   tambourine

   Group 1:   jingle bells
   Group 2:   wood block

2. Put an extended pattern on the board with repeat bars. (The length of the pattern should depend on the maturity of the class):

Read and clap the pattern. Put an ostinato on the board directly under the first pattern. Read and thump (knuckles on desk) the pattern.

Divide the class and read both parts. Select individuals to read and clap the patterns. Select individuals to play both parts on different sounding rhythm instruments.

3. The last activity can be developed into a highly integrated lesson, as shown in the next chart. You will find many other songs that can be developed in the same manner. Begin with simple and familiar songs and let the children decide what to use as an ostinato.

4. Proceed to the next chart.

Scotland's Burning

Traditional Round

Scotland's burning, Scotland's burning,

Look out! Look out! Fire! fire! fire! fire!

Pour on wa-ter, Pour on wa-ter.

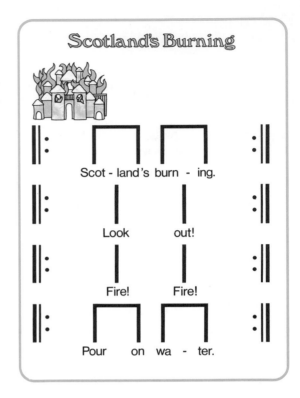

Scotland's Burning

Scot - land's burn - ing.

Look out!

Fire! Fire!

Pour on wa - ter.

PREPARATION FOR THE CHART

1. Teach the song.
2. Sing the song, using previous rhythmic experiences (see Chart 11).

INTRODUCE THE CHART

1. Read the words with the class, using the repeat bars.
2. Teacher sings the first measure, class sings the repeat without losing the beat (echo).
3. Continue this activity throughout the entire chart without losing the beat.
4. Sing the entire song, starting softly (*piano, p*), building up to "Fire! Fire!" (*forte, f*), and getting softer on "Pour on water" (*mezzo-piano, mp*).

5. If the children are familiar with dynamic markings (*p, f*), you might introduce *crescendo* (gradually getting louder) and *decrescendo* (gradually getting softer). The musical symbols for them are:

   crescendo $<$ decrescendo $>$

   [*Note: These can be related to the mathematical symbols greater than ($<$) and lesser than ($>$).*]

6. Select one line of the song to be an ostinato. Divide the class. Have Group 1 start the ostinato and establish the beat. Then have Group 2 begin singing the song, coming in on the beat.

   [*Note: When introducing this activity, it is recommended that you point to the rhythm symbols of the ostinato selected on the chart.*]

As the children become more confident, divide the class into five groups. Have one group sing the song, while the other four are ostinatos. Encourage the children to follow the words and rhythm symbols on the chart with their eyes while singing.

Suggest that their voices must fit the words in tone color and volume (loud and soft).

OTHER SONGS TO USE

"Are You Sleeping?" • "Chi-Chi-Pa-Pa" • "Who Has the Penny?"

ADDITIONAL ACTIVITIES

Form

1. Sing the song and dramatize the melodic contour. Does the melody start high or low? (low) Does the melody move up or down? (up)

   "Scotland's burning" ↗ ↗

What happens when we sing "Look out!"?
(the melody moves upward slightly)

"Look out!" ⌐ ⌐

Is "Fire! Fire!" high or low? (high)
Does "Fire! Fire!" move at all? (no)

Fire! Fire! — — — —

Does the melody for "Pour on water" sound familiar? (It's the same as the first phrase, "Scotland's burning.")

"Pour on water" ⌐⌐

2. Draw a picture of the melody in the air with large arm movements. Then have the class put the melody on the chalkboard or large pieces of paper in the same fashion. Sing the song while making a picture of the melody. (There will be many variations. Accept those that give a conceptual approach to **melodic contour.**)

Melodic contour

||: Scotland's burning :|| ⌐⌐⌐

||: Look out! :|| / / /

||: Fire! Fire! :|| — — — —

||: Pour on water :|| ⌐⌐⌐

3. Give letter names to each phrase. If two phrases are alike, give them the same letter (musical form):

Scotland's burning—A
Look out!—B
Fire! Fire!—C
Pour on water—A

4. Use the last activity on musical form with other familiar songs. You will find a direct relationship to language development in such areas as phrasing • sequence • similarities/differences • visual and aural acuity and perception.

Instruments

1. Read the chart and play each phrase on a different instrument.

   A. Scotland's burning—sticks and/or woodblock
   B. Look out!—tambourines or jingle sticks
   C. Fire! Fire!—cymbals or drum
   A. Pour on water—sticks or woodblock

   The reason for using the same instrumentation on the first and last phrase is to reinforce the concept of musical form.
2. Create an original ostinato for instruments while you sing the song. Put the pattern on the board.

Round

1. Sing the song as a round in two, three, or four parts, depending on the maturity of your class.
2. Step the pattern of the song as a round. For the more mature children, divide the class into two, three, or four groups. Sing the song as a round and step or walk the pattern, and turn the phrase. This activity can be done in circles:

Group 1
Group 2
Group 3

Psychomotor Development and Perception

1. Can the children maintain a rhythmic ostinato on instruments?
2. Can the children maintain a melodic ostinato or sing a round in two, three, or four parts?

Aural Acuity and Perception

1. Can the children recognize similarities and differences in phrases and melodic contour?
2. Can the children distinguish loud and soft? Phrasing? Low and high?

Visual Acuity and Perception

1. Can the children visualize a melody by gross and fine motor activities? Melodic contour on the chalkboard or paper?
2. Can the children sing the song from the chart and use the repeat marks without losing the beat?

Echo

PREPARATION FOR THE CHART

The three preceding charts presented the differences between **beat** and **pattern.** The beat being steady and the pattern having long and short sounds and silence. The succeeding charts develop this concept further through visual perception (reading the pattern) and motor perception (writing the pattern).

INTRODUCE THE CHART

1. Tell the class to feel a beat inside of them before you start the chart. Start this beat by moving your hand up and down. When you clap the first line of the chart, the children are to echo you without losing the beat.

   Teacher claps   Class echoes

Continue through the entire chart, keeping the beat and getting the complete feeling of the rest.

2. Choose one child to be the leader and clap the chart while the class echoes.
3. Clap the chart and give each pattern a different tone quality which the class must echo:

—clap softly (*p*)
—knuckles on desk
—clap loudly (*f*)
—fingertips on desk (*p*)

4. Clap the chart and call on individual children to be the echo.
5. Clap the chart, class echoes, and then says the rhythm syllables:

Teacher claps and children echo   Children say

ta ta ta rest
ti–ti ti–ti ta rest
ta ti–ti ta ta
ta ta ta rest

ADDITIONAL ACTIVITIES

Dictation

Pass our paper and fold into fourths. On the chalkboard, draw a square divided into four sections, each section being numbered.

1.	2.
3.	4.

Teacher claps   Children clap

1.
2.
3.
4.

Children say   Children write

ta ta   ta ta
ta ti–ti ta   ta
ta ta   ta rest
ta rest ti–ti ta

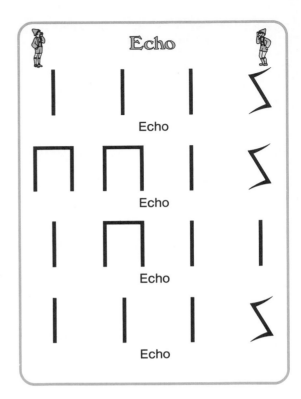

Choose individual children to fill in the squares on the chalkboard. How many children wrote the pattern correctly? This activity should be done many times throughout the year.

Extended Patterns

1. Ask individual children to clap a four beat pattern (| | ⊓ |). The class will echo clap and say the rhythm syllables. The leader will then write the pattern on the chalkboard and draw a measure line (|). Choose another child to clap a pattern for the class to echo. Have him write his pattern next to the first one and draw a measure line.

(| | ⊓ | | ⊓ ⊓ | | |)

Continue this activity for four measures, each pattern being different:

॥ । । ⊓ । | ⊓ ⊓ ⊓ । । | । ₹ ⊓ । | । । । ₹ ‖

Note: At this time, introduce the double bar which means the end of the pattern (or song). This is like a period at the end of a sentence (‖).

2. Clap the entire four measures. These four-measure patterns can be put on a chart or long strips of tagboard. As the class becomes more confident, encourage them to make longer phrases or to make rhythm patterns of mystery songs with original illustrations. Be sure to make corrections, if necessary, before presenting the songs to the class. The original charts can be song fragments or the entire song:

Song Fragment
"Twinkle Twinkle"

Entire Song
"Hot Cross Buns"

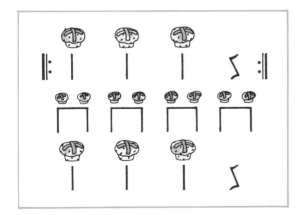

3. *Canon.* It has been said that "*all* rounds are canons but not *all* canons are rounds." A canon is a rhythmic or tonal passage done in two or more parts, each beginning at a different time.

Note: Canon clapping is a highly integrated activity which requires the aural and visual concentration needed to encourage children to read a written score. A rhythm canon can be written on the chalkboard and clapped or played on rhythm instruments, much like singing a round.

To introduce the canon to the children in the lower grades, (1) read and clap the entire pattern; (2) teacher begins clapping the pattern; (3) children begin clapping the pattern, after the teacher has completed the first measure:

Jingle Bells
⊓ । ₹ ⊓ । ₹

Ten Little Indians
। ⊓ । ⊓ । ⊓ । ।

Three Blind Mice
। । । ₹ । । । ₹

Encourage the children to illustrate other familiar songs or poems and to write the rhythm patterns. These can be done on large chart paper and used by the entire class.

Teacher: । ।   ⊓ । | ⊓ ⊓ । । | । ₹ ⊓ । | । । । ₹ :‖

Children: । । ⊓ । | ⊓ ⊓ । । | । ₹ ⊓ । | । । । ₹ :‖

Divide the class into two groups. Group 1 begins clapping; as soon as they have clapped one measure, Group 2 begins. (Do not expect complete success at first with canon clapping.)

OTHER SONGS TO USE

1. Write the pattern of themes or fragments of familiar songs on the board. Clap the pattern and identify the song.
2. Write the pattern of song fragments on a chart. Put illustrations of the songs on the chart and match the rhythm pattern to the illustration. For example, using "Ten Little Indians," "Three Blind Mice," and "Jingle Bells":

EVALUATION OF RHYTHMIC AND PERCEPTUAL SKILLS

Psychomotor Development and Perception

1. Can the children hear a rhythm pattern and write it on the chalkboard?
2. Can they perform dual activities: left hand/right hand, balance and laterality?

Aural and Visual Acuity

1. Can the children listen to one pattern and feel the beat while clapping or playing a different pattern (canon)?
2. Are they becoming increasingly aware of the silent beat (₹)?
3. Can the children read extended patterns?

37

16

Low and High

For example,

piano—"down" is left and "up" is right
cello and double bass—"down" is high
  and "up" is low
clarinet and saxophone—"down" is low

2. Teach the song.
3. Sing the song and clap the pattern.

Note: The half note (♩) will be introduced on a later chart. For this lesson, teach the half note by rote. The half note is held for two beats, clap the first beat and hold the second beat.

4. Sing the song and use previous rhythm experiences. Clap the beat • step or walk the beat • walk the beat and turn the phrase.
5. Sing the song and dramatize the melodic contour. When the melody is "low," bend down. When the melody is "high," stretch up tall with arms held high.

PREPARATION FOR THE CHART

Note: The concept of high and low pitch is a very abstract idea for children to conceive. To many children, "low" means soft and "high" means loud. This concept often follows through to the upper grades, as any teacher of glee clubs and choruses knows so well.

1. To develop the concept of "high" and "low" and "loud" and "soft," use the language arts or story approach. One example of this is the sound of a siren on a fire engine heard in the distance, coming closer and closer and then fading away. This exercise is invaluable to the child who has not yet learned to use his voice to create differences in pitch.

Note: It is not advisable to use the "down" and "up" terminology, because many instruments do not follow this rule.

INTRODUCE THE CHART

Note: Take out the resonator or song bells.

1. Point to the low bell on the chart. How low can the children make their voices (sound, not sing)? Imitate the low bell (Bong).
2. Point to the high bell. How high can the children make their voices? Imitate the high bell (Ting).
3. Imitate the "sound" of the bells and dramatize the "low" and "high" sounds with body motions.
4. Can the children make the "low" sound soft and then loud? (This is called **crescendo** and is symbolized as ⟨.)
5. Can the children make the "high" sound loud and then soft? (This is called **decrescendo** and is symbolized as ⟩.)

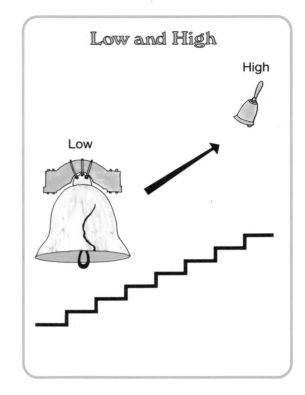

Low and High

High

Low

6. Sing or play a low note (middle C) on the bells or piano. Sing a neutral syllable on this note and have the children match the tone with their voices ("ah" or "oh" with a relaxed jaw will give a good, full sound).
7. Sing or play the high note (C octave). Using a neutral syllable, sing the high note. Move from "high" to "low" several times and see if the children can match the tone.
8. Play a rhythm pattern on the bells or piano, moving from low to high. Have the children echo the pattern:

low	high	low, low	high

high	low, low	high	low

Eleanor Kidd

Do you hear the bells ring - ing in the sky?

Fill - ing the air with their song so high.

Lis - ten to the big bell sing his song.

Lis - ten to the small bell sing a - long.

One sings high and one sings low.

See how the bells swing to and fro.

ADDITIONAL ACTIVITIES

1. Sing the song and make a picture in the air of the melodic contour. Use large arm movements. Later, make a picture of the melody on paper or the chalkboard.

   Note: There will be many variations on this concept. Accept those that show an awareness of the melodic line.

2. Play the melody on the bells or piano as an accompaniment to the song.

3. If you have resonator bells, pass out the bells from Middle C to the C above. Can the children play the melody? When you introduce this activity, it would be wise to give each child a signal when he is to play. Later, they will be able to play the melody without a conductor, using their sense of rhythm and pitch to guide them.

EVALUATION OF RHYTHMIC AND PERCEPTUAL SKILLS

Psychomotor Development and Perception

1. Can the children dramatize the melodic contour of a song?
2. Can they draw the melodic contour in the air, on the chalkboard, or on paper?

Aural Acuity and Perception

1. Can the children identify higher and lower pitches?
2. Can they identify and differentiate ascending and descending melodies?
3. Can they differentiate and produce vocally louder and softer tones (crescendo and decrescendo)?

9. Point to the stairs on the chart. Tell the children that melodies (songs) sometimes move in a stepwise fashion.

   Note: You may wish to play the C scale on the bells or piano to establish the stepwise concept.

10. Point to the stairs on the chart and sing low C to high C, stepwise, on a neutral syllable (loo).
11. Sing "Bells" or any other song using a stepwise melody within an octave range.

Point to the stairs on the chart while singing the song, moving from "low" to "high" with the melody.

12. Choose a leader to point to the chart while the class sings the song.

OTHER SONGS TO USE

"Taffy" • "Do, Re, Mi" • "For Health and Strength" (use of low ti).

17

Sol-Mi

Sol

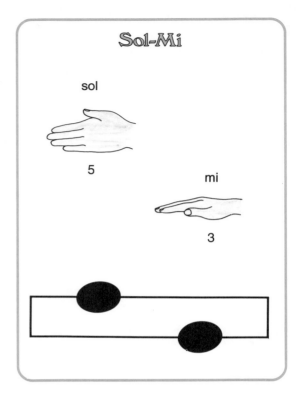

Sol-Mi

sol

5

mi

3

[Note: *Although this is the first exposure to the sol–mi on a chart, it is hoped that you have used the roll call on sol–mi with the class since the beginning of the school year. Naturally, this would be taught by rote.*

To the teacher with little musical training, there are several ways to find a minor third. On the piano or bells, from G down to E or from the lowest of three black notes to the black note below it:

Another way to find a minor third is to count three half-steps down. The only natural half-steps are between E and F, and B and C. The other half-steps are between white and black notes.

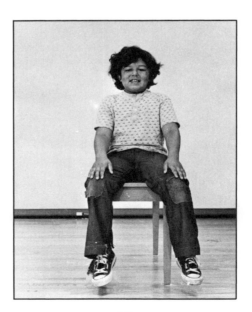

Mi

Sol can begin on any note of the scale and mi is always three half steps lower (minor third). This is important for the child who cannot match your sol–mi but sings a minor third either lower or higher. Match your sol–mi to his pitch so he will not feel embarrassment. Sol–mi will be notated as s–m after being introduced.]

PREPARATION FOR THE CHART

The sol–mi (minor third) is the natural chant of children around the world. Children hailing their friends or calling their pets use the minor third or sol–mi.

1. Ask someone in the class to pretend he is calling his friend who is far down the

street. "John–ny" is usually called by chanting "sol–mi." If the first child you call on does not use the minor third to call a friend, call on others until someone does.

2. Ask someone in the class to coax a little kitten to come to them. "Here kitty, kitty, kitty" will usually be "sol mi–mi, mi–mi, mi–mi." Will the tone of voice be the same when calling the kitten as when calling Johnny?

3. Teach the arm signal for sol, which is made by clapping at chest level while sitting in a chair or on the floor.

4. Teach the arm signal for mi, which is made by slapping the knees or upper leg.

[Note: "Mi is me" seems to help children understand the descending minor third and gives a contrasting sound.]

5. Walk from child to child and sing his name with sol–mi, using arm signals. The child will echo you, singing his name and using arm signals. Adapt the tone syllables to the syllabication of the names.

6. Go around the room and sing each child's name with arm signals. The class echoes you, singing the child's name, using arm signals, then the individual child sings his name, using arm signals.

[Note: This activity is especially effective for the child who needs peer recognition. Move quickly from one child to another in order to avoid any embarrassment for the insecure child. Be sure to insist upon arm signals for sol–mi.]

7. Call the roll by singing each child's name on sol–mi. The child answers "I'm here" on sol–mi with arm signals. If someone is absent, encourage the class to sing "He's not here," on sol–mi. Try to keep the beat while doing this activity.

INTRODUCE THE CHART

[Note: Arm and hand singing is an integral part of the Threshold to Music program. These signals are illustrated on the charts, but arm signals are combined with rhythmic activities as they provide a more active participation on the part of the child. Hand signals and arm-singing instructions for other tone syllables of the diatonic scale will be introduced on later charts. The use of both hand and arm signals will give children an understanding of the intervals used to create a scale. Photographs of hand signals can be found in the Appendix.]

Hold your hand over the hand signal for "sol" on the chart. Sing "sol." The children will echo you and make the hand sign for sol. Sing "Here is sol" while pointing to the chart. The class will echo, "There is sol." Point to "mi" on the chart and sing, "Here is mi." The class will echo, "There is mi."

SONGS TO USE

Tap out the pattern of familiar songs using sol–mi on the chart with hand signals. For example,

"This Old Man"

⊓ | ⊓ |
s m s s m s

"Bluebird, Bluebird"

| | | |
s m s m

"Rain, Rain Go Away"

| | ⊓ |
s m s s m

ADDITIONAL ACTIVITIES

1. Make flash cards of various rhythm patterns using sol–mi:

| | ⊓ | | |
s m m s m

⊓ | ⊓ |
s m s s m s

| | ⊓ |
s s m m s

Establish the pitch for "sol." Hold up a flash card and have the class sing the pattern, using hand or arm signals.

2. Use the flash cards with individual children, letting them establish their own pitch for sol.

3. Ask questions using sol–mi and hand or arm signals, and let individual children answer with sol–mi and hand or arm signals:

Teacher: "Ma-ry, where's your book?"
| | ⊓ |
s m s s m

Mary: "In the clo-set."
| | | |
s m s m

4. Establish the pitch for sol. Using your hand over the hand signals on the chart, indicate various rhythm patterns using sol–mi, but *do not* sing. Can the children sing the patterns you have indicated? Ask one child to be the leader. Let him establish the pitch for sol and indicate the patterns on the chart.

5. Write the **diatonic scale** with tone syllables on the board or on a chart for future use. Number the syllables from one to eight:

do	re	mi	fa	sol	la	ti	do
1	2	3	4	5	6	7	8

Point to sol. What number is "sol" on the scale? (5)
Point to mi. What number is "mi" on the scale? (3)

This can also be done vertically to reinforce low and high and the position of various intervals on the scale.

do	8
ti	7
la	6
sol	5
fa	4
mi	3
re	2
do	1

6. Point to the two line staff at the bottom of the chart.

[*Note: The use of the two line staff on the chart is to prepare the children for the complete staff in a developmental manner.*]

• Tell the children that sol is *around* a line and mi is *around* the line below sol. (It is recommended to use "around" the line rather than "on" the line, as in handwriting.)

• The pitch for sol can start on any note of the scale, wherever it is comfortable for you and the class. Encourage the children to take a deep breath, open their mouths, and relax their jaws when they sing "sol." This will produce a beautiful tone: As long as your hand is over the sol, the children will hold the tone, taking a breath whenever they feel the need. Do not *push* the tone by running out of air. Try singing sol softly and then get louder:

$<$ crescendo   decrescendo $>$

7. Hold your hand over the mi on the chart, dropping your voice down to show the interval of a minor third. Sing "mi" with the hand sign. The children will echo with the hand sign.

Tell the children to take a deep breath and smile without clenching the teeth, when they sing "mi." Hold the mi as long as your hand is over the mi on the chart. Sing "mi" with **dynamics** ($< >$).

8. Indicate various rhythm patterns on the chart, using hand signals for sol–mi. The children will sing the patterns with hand signals. For example,

```
|  |  ⊓  |
s  m  s  s  m
```

```
⊓  |  ⊓  |
s s  m  s s  m
```

[*Note: If your class has difficulty conceptualizing the interval of the minor third, the above activity can be done with arm signals. The more mature children will enjoy using hand signals (see p. 95).*

Until the children are confident in singing "sol–mi," begin these activities with the descending minor third (sol–mi) as the ascending minor third (mi–sol) is sometimes difficult for children in the lower grades.]

9. Draw two lines on the floor, about one foot apart.
Choose one, two, or three children:

Teacher sings:	Class echoes with arm signals:
s m s m	s m s m

Children jump from sol line to mi line:

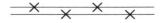

Teacher sings:	Class echoes with arm signals:
m s s m	m s s m

Children jump from mi line to sol line:

EVALUATION OF RHYTHMIC AND PERCEPTUAL SKILLS

Psychomotor Development and Perception

Can the children dramatize the descending minor third with such motor activities as arm singing, hand singing, and body motion?

Aural Acuity and Perception

1. Can the majority of the class match the sol–mi with their voices?
2. Can the children recognize the minor third (sol–mi) in a familiar song?

Visual Acuity and Perception

Can the children recognize the descending minor third on a two line staff?

The Whole Rest

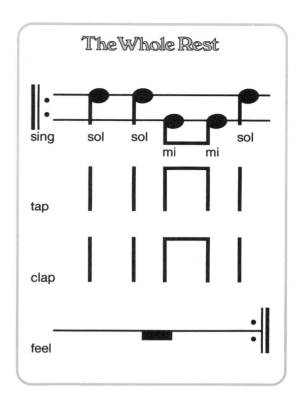

PREPARATION FOR THE CHART

To prepare the children for the chart use previous rhythmic experiences and hand or arm singing:

- echo clapping
- inner hearing
- echo singing on sol–mi, using either hand or arm signals.
- roll call

INTRODUCE THE CHART

1. Choose one child to read and clap the rhythm pattern of the first line while stepping the beat. Continue through the chart until you come to the last line.

2. Ask the children how many beats they feel for each line when they clap the pattern and step the beat. How many steps did they take for each line (4)?

3. Tell the children the last line is the symbol for the whole rest and make a rest motion for each beat.

   [Note: The children will remember the whole rest when you tell them that the whole rest gets the greatest number of beats and therefore, "hangs" from the line (▬).]

4. Establish the pitch for "sol," and sing the first line with hand or arm signals.

5. Continue through the chart with clapping, tapping, and feeling. Observe the repeat sign. Did the children retain the pitch (sol) while doing the other activities?

6. Choose one child to read and sing the chart, using hand signals, without losing the beat. Did he retain the pitch for sol?

7. Repeat the chart several times, increasing the speed with each repetition.

   *[Note: If your class is building up a musical vocabulary, add the term **accelerando**. Liken it to a gas pedal on a car (accelerator). The children will immediately see the relationship.]*

ADDITIONAL ACTIVITIES

1. Choose one child to clap an original pattern and write it on the board:

   ⊓ ⊓ | |

Ask another child to place the syllables of his choice under the pattern, using the letters s and m.

s s m m s s

Sing the pattern, using arm signals.

2. Ask the children to compose their own rhythm pattern on sol–mi. Write them on large pieces of paper to present to the class.
3. Make flash cards for clap, tap, feel, step, and the whole rest:

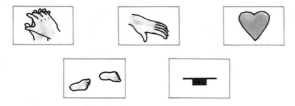

Write a sol–mi rhythm pattern on the board and use the flash cards with it.

4. Use this chart or flash cards to give children a break in the regular school day. This is especially effective when used to refresh a tired class. Some other charts to use for this purpose are "Inner Hearing," "Rhythms," and "Scotland's Burning."

EVALUATION OF RHYTHMIC AND PERCEPTUAL SKILLS

Psychomotor Development and Perception

Can the children recognize and feel silence while keeping the beat (whole rest)?

Aural Acuity and Perception

Can the children retain a given pitch while engaging in diverse motor activities?

Toy Symphony

The ability to listen plays a very important role in a child's total learning program. This is a skill that should be taught in much the same manner as reading readiness and number concepts. Too often the child (and teacher) is besieged with background sounds (i.e., music in the grocery store, dentist office, etc.). As a result, this part of the child's musical experience has often been misused, abused, or neglected completely.

Many people do not realize the wonderful ways in which symphonies, concertos, and even simple songs are constructed. It is exciting to listen for repetition of themes and rhythms, changing keys, and instrumental

entries. With the understanding of the architecture of music comes an even greater appreciation and, thus, true enjoyment.

Not every classroom teacher or all the children in a class are going to be able to hear and understand all the complex parts of a composition, but it is possible to hear and identify many new things.

[Note: In order to use this chart you will need a recording of the "Toy Symphony." Contact the Music Department for assistance in finding the record.]

PREPARATION FOR THE CHART

1. Tell the children the story of Joseph Haydn.

Joseph Haydn was born in Austria in 1732, the same year as George Washington. (Find Austria on a map or globe. Subtract 1732 from this year. How long ago was Joseph Haydn born?) When Haydn was five years old, he was sent to a neighboring village to study music. When he was eight years old, he left for the large city of Vienna to sing in a church choir. Many times he would be hungry, but he always kept his happy disposition. He studied hard and began to write music when he was seventeen years old.

One day, a wealthy prince, Prince Esterhazy, hired him as a music master. The prince had a large castle with many rooms and everyone who worked for him lived in the castle. It was Haydn's duty to teach the musicians and keep them in practice so they would be ready to play for concerts, at mealtimes, and for dancing. In addition to composing all the music, he also had to see that the musicians behaved politely and wore clean clothes and powdered wigs.

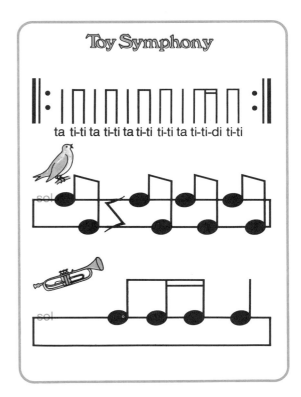

Haydn once went to a toy fair and was so delighted with the music-making toys he wanted to buy them, even though he had no children of his own. After all, his own musicians called him "Papa," so why shouldn't he compose a little symphony using the toy instruments?

The only real instruments used in the "Toy Symphony" are violins and bass viols. Instead of woodwinds, he used bird whistles —the cuckoo and the trilling nightingale. For brasses, he used the tin trumpets; and for percussion, a triangle, a rattle, and a tin drum.

2. Introduce pictures of the string family. Can the children identify the violin and

bass viol (sometimes called bass fiddle)? Which instrument will have a high voice? Is it large or small? Which instrument will have a low voice? Is it large or small?

3. If you have an instrumental program in your school, invite some of the upper grade children to demonstrate playing the stringed instruments.

4. Play the first movement of a recording of the "Toy Symphony."

• Did the children recognize the cuckoo and the nightingale? • How did the tin trumpet sound? • Can they imitate the sound and pattern of the tin trumpet? • Ask one child to clap the pattern of the trumpet.

INTRODUCE THE CHART

1. Read and clap the rhythm syllables at the top of the chart. Do the children notice something new (⎕⎕ ti ti–di)?

[Note: These (ti–di) are sixteenth notes and should be taught by rote for now. They will be developed further in Level 2. There are two sixteenth notes to each eighth note, so naturally they will be twice as fast.]

Be sure to observe the repeat signs without losing the beat. Play the first section and see if the children can identify the theme, using rhythm syllables.

2. Clap the pattern of the "cuckoo," and then sing the pattern using hand signals.

[Note: If you are using hand signals as presented in Chart 17, make the motion for the rest with one hand.]

Continue playing the record and identify the "cuckoo" with hand signals.

3. Clap the pattern of the tin trumpet, using the rhythm syllables for the sixteenth notes (⎕⎕ I, ti ti–di ta). Now sing the pattern with hand signals. (Maintaining the same pitch can sometimes present a problem.) Play the record and identify the trumpet with hand signals.

4. Play the entire first movement and identify the parts on the chart.

ADDITIONAL ACTIVITIES

1. Play the record and let the children count how many times they hear the theme for the "cuckoo."

2. Divide the class. Have one group make the hand signals for the "cuckoo" theme, and the other group clap the pattern of the "tin trumpet," while listening to the record.

3. Another listening activity is to have the children sit absolutely silent for three minutes. How many sounds did they hear? A bird? An automobile horn? Footsteps?

EVALUATION OF RHYTHMIC AND PERCEPTUAL SKILLS

Psychomotor Development and Perception

Can the children relate the interval of the descending minor third (sol–mi) with hand signals. (This will depend upon the maturity of your class.)

Aural and Visual Acuity and Perception

1. Can the children listen and identify different themes?

2. Can the children read a pattern and identify the theme being played?

I've a Pair of ...

Jewish Folk Song

I've a pair of fish - es, fish - es,

They are wash-ing dish - es, dish - es.

This is in - deed a won - der,

See the fish - es wash-ing dish - es.

'Tis in-deed a won-der,'Tis in-deed a won-der.

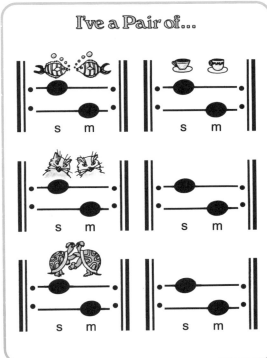

I've a Pair of...

s   m   s   m

s   m   s   m

s   m   s   m

PREPARATION FOR CHART

1. Teach the song.
2. Sing the song and clap the pattern.
3. Sing the song and step the pattern except for "fishes" and "dishes" (sol–mi). Sing and use arm signals for sol–mi.
4. At another time, use the song as a mystery song. Ask one child to be the leader, clapping the pattern and using arm signals for the sol–mi.

INTRODUCE THE CHART

1. Point to the chart and sing the sol–mi with the repeats. (How long did it take the children to identify the song?)

2. Choose one child to point to the chart while the class sings the song, keeping the beat on sol–mi with arm signals ("fishes" and "dishes").
3. Tell the children they will have to create new verses—the more absurd the better.

   [Note: Encourage imagery, rhyming, and consonant development. For example,

   kittens knitting mittens
   turtles jumping hurdles
   (wearing girdles)
   guppies bark like puppies]

4. This is a cumulative song and can have as many verses as the children can create.

[You will find that children in the lower grades will respond well to repetition. While the song may seem interminable to you, as a teacher, the insecure child is often listening and waiting to become an active participant. Cumulative songs will give this child an opportunity to develop a positive attitude toward himself in relationship to music.]

5. Put the rhyming words on the chalkboard or on a large chart for future use. Sing the song, using arm signals for sol–mi.
6. Ask one child to lead the song by keeping the beat and pointing to the sol–mi's on the chart whenever they occur in the song.

ADDITIONAL ACTIVITIES

1. Draw two lines on the floor and ask several children to jump or hop the sol–mi everytime they hear the interval in the song. (Remember to keep the beat.)
2. Give the G and E resonator bells to one child. As the class sings the song, read the chart, and have the child play the minor third (sol–mi) when it occurs in the song.
3. Use different rhythm instruments for each verse:

   > fishes—triangle
   > kittens—jingle bells
   > turtles—wood block

4. Encourage the class to create their own illustrations for a classroom chart.
5. Use the song for class dictation. Clap the pattern by phrases. For example,

	Class claps	
Teacher claps	with syllables	Class writes
⊓ ⊓ I I I I	ti–ti ti–ti ta ta ta ta	⊓ ⊓ I I I I

EVALUATION OF RHYTHMIC AND PERCEPTUAL SKILLS

Psychomotor Development and Perception

Can the children dramatize the descending minor third with gross motor motions?

Aural Acuity and Perception

Are the children becoming increasingly aware of the descending minor third (sol–mi)?

Musical Development and Social Maturity

1. Can the children create their own verses?
2. Can the children relate to the absurd with enjoyment and humor?

Clap Your Hands

Teacher
Can you sing on one note?
┌─┐ ┌─┐ │ │
s s s s s s

Class
We can sing on one note.
┌─┐ ┌─┐ │ │
s s s s s s

Teacher
Can you sing on this note?
┌─┐ ┌─┐ │ │
m m m m m m

Class
We can sing on this note.
┌─┐ ┌─┐ │ │
m m m m m m

Teacher   Class
This is sol.   This is sol.
┌─┐ │   ┌─┐ │
s s s   s s s

Teacher   Class
This is mi.   This is mi.
┌─┐ │   ┌─┐ │
m m m   m m m

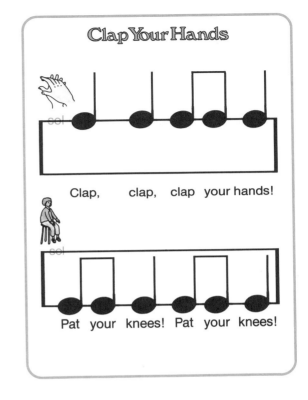

Clap Your Hands

Clap,   clap,   clap your hands!

Pat your knees! Pat your knees!

[Note: The next two charts emphasize the fact that a tone can be repeated. As long as the note is around the same line, the tone is the same. This may cause some difficulties at first because of the natural tendency to sing the minor third (sol–mi). Because these charts teach the same basic concept, the "Evaluation of Rhythmic and Perceptual Skills" appears at the end of Chart 22.]

PREPARATION FOR THE CHART

Sing a rhythmic question on sol with hand or arm signals. Longer sentences can be used to dramatize and reinforce the concept of a repeated tone.

INTRODUCE THE CHART

1. Choose one child to clap the rhythm pattern of the first line with rhythm syllables. The class will echo if he is correct and be silent if he is incorrect.
2. Choose another child to clap the rhythm pattern of the second line with rhythm syllables. The class will echo if he is correct.
3. Read the words on the chart. Clap the pattern of the words.
4. Establish the pitch for sol. Chant: "Here is sol. Who can sing the first line?" Choose one child to sing the first line with arm signals. The class will echo.

5. Sing the chant on mi. Chant: "Here is mi. Who can sing the second line?" Choose one child to sing the second line with arm signals. The class will echo.
6. The class will then sing the entire chart with arm signals and tone syllables (sol–mi).

   [Note: To prepare the children and establish the beat, begin by saying "One–two–ready–sing."]

7. Sing the entire chart with the words and arm signals.
8. Ask for volunteers to read and sing the entire chart.
9. Turn to the next chart.

Here Is Sol—
Where Is Mi?

[Note: This chart is used to develop the concept of movable "do," which is the basis of **solmization** (tone syllables) in the Threshold to Music. This concept (introduced in the "Early Childhood" charts) should be presented after the children are confident with the interval of the minor third (sol–mi). It is not necessary to pitch the sol on any absolute note, such as G. "Sol" may be any pitch within the vocal or instrumental range. The hand on the chart represents the five lines of the musical staff.]

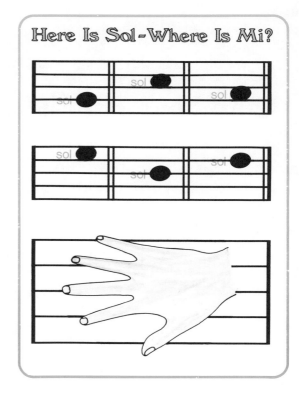

Here Is Sol—Where Is Mi?

1. Ask the children, "If sol is around a line, where is mi?" (Mi is around the line below sol. Use the word "around" rather than "on" the line. This will eliminate confusion with writing words.)
2. Ask the children, "If sol is in a space, where is mi?" (Mi is in the space below sol.)

INTRODUCE THE CHART

1. Point to the staff on the chart. How many lines do the children see (five lines)? How many spaces do they see (four spaces)? Number the lines, starting at the bottom, 1 through 5.
2. Point to each measure on the chart and ask individual children to find the mi. For example, ask "If sol is around the second line, where is mi?" The child will answer, "Mi is around the first line," and then come up to the chart to locate the mi on the staff.
3. Point to the chart and sing the "sol" on varying pitches. Ask individual children to come up to the chart and point to the line or space for "mi" and sing the minor third below "sol."
4. Choose individual children to be the leader and sing the sol and point to the chart. This child may choose someone to come up and sing the mi and find the note on the chart.

   [Note: Be sure the pitch varies with the position of the note on the staff. Sol on the second line will be lower in pitch than sol on the fourth space, even though the pitch is not absolute.]

5. Place your hand over the hand on the chart. Grasp one finger. This is to rein-

force the fact that the note goes "around" the line. Sing "Here is sol" on one note:

Then sing "Where is mi?" a minor third below:

Ask one child to show where mi is by grasping the finger below. When the child correctly identifies the position of mi, he sings "Here is mi."

6. Vary the fingers and the pitch for sol and have the class sing the mi. Use the spaces by placing the sol between the fingers, remembering to raise and lower the pitch as shown on the chart.

ADDITIONAL ACTIVITIES

1. Move from child to child and hold out your hand with the fingers spread apart. Teacher sings "sol is here, where is mi?" on one pitch, grasping a finger:

Child sings, "mi is here," grasping the finger below.

Teacher sings, "sol is here, where is mi?" on a different pitch and uses a space:

Child sings the minor third, "mi is here," identifying the space:

2. Use mirror image and have the children identify sol and mi on their own hands as they sing the minor third. When they are confident of the minor third, ask a child to be the leader.

EVALUATION OF RHYTHMIC AND PERCEPTUAL SKILLS

Aural and Visual Acuity and Perception

1. Can the children reproduce the repeated note with their voices?
2. Can they read the charts and reproduce the tones of the minor third?
3. Can they recognize and sing mi on various pitches?

Up and Down

[Note: Charts 23, 24, and 25 reinforce the descending minor third. Draw the children's attention to the fact that sol is in a space on the staff and mi is in the space below sol. The Evaluation for these charts appears after Chart 25.]

INTRODUCE THE CHART

1. Establish the pitch for sol. Sing the first line with arm or hand signals and tone syllables.
2. Ask one child to lead the class singing the first line with arm signals and tone syllables.
3. Sing the first line, using the words.
4. Ask one child to sing the second line with tone syllables and arm signals. If he sings it correctly, the class will echo, if he is incorrect, they will remain silent.
5. Sing the second line, using words and arm signals.

6. Sing the entire chart with arm or hand signals; dramatize the minor third by standing tall for "sol" and stooping for "mi."

ADDITIONAL ACTIVITIES

1. Establish the pitch for sol. Teacher sings various rhythm patterns using sol and mi with arm signals.

Teacher sings	Class echoes
❘ ⊓ ❘ ❘	❘ ⊓ ❘ ❘
s m m s m	s m m s m
❘ ₹ ⊓ ❘	❘ ₹ ⊓ ❘
s s s m	s s s m

For the more mature class, start the pattern on "mi":

Teacher sings	Class echoes
❘ ❘ ⊓ ❘	❘ ❘ ⊓ ❘
m s m m s	m s m m s

2. Establish the pitch for sol. Teacher makes the arm signals but *does not* sing. Class sings the pattern with arm signals. This activity can also be done with hand signals.

3. Make individual staff charts on heavy paper and cut out notes of black paper. Distribute the staff and notes to the children. Designate on which line or space the sol will be.

Teacher sings with hand signals	Children echo and place notes
❘ ❘ ⊓ ❘	❘ ❘ ⊓ ❘
s m s s m	s m s s m

Up and Down

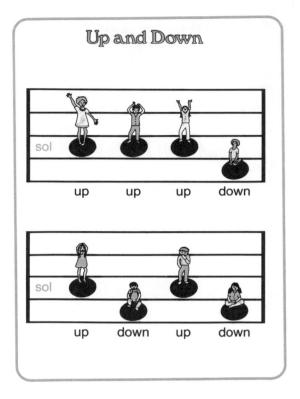

sol			
up	up	up	down

sol			
up	down	up	down

Use many variations of rhythm patterns containing sol–mi. You can also put the staff on the chalk board and let the children write the pattern after it is sung.

4. Variation of the above activity. Establish the position of sol.

Hand signals without singing	Class sings and places notes
❘ ❘ ⊓ ❘	❘ ❘ ⊓ ❘
s s m m s	s s m m s

5. Play various patterns on the recorder, bells, or piano. Establish the position of "sol." Have class sing the pattern with hand signals and place notes on their staff charts.
6. Turn to the next chart.

Mystery Songs

Measures 1–8: The bluebird flies in and out the windows, keeping the beat.

Measures 9–14: "Bluebird" taps a partner and two "bluebirds" fly through the windows.

Measures 15–16: The first "bluebird" takes his place in the circle and the second "bluebird" is in the center.

Repeat the game.

PREPARATION FOR THE CHART

BLUEBIRD, BLUEBIRD

Teach both verses of the song. The names can be changed to fit the "bluebird" in your class. (Oh, Barbara, aren't you tired?)

1. Teach the singing game.

Formation: Single circle with joined hands held high to make the windows. One child in the center as the "bluebird."

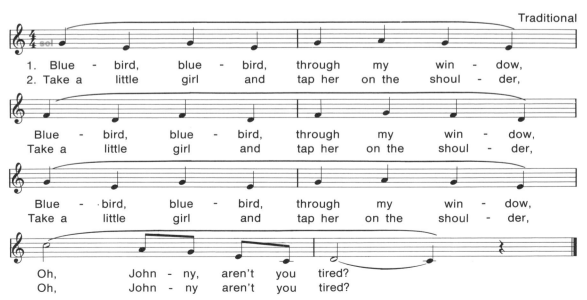

Traditional

1. Blue - bird, blue - bird, through my win - dow,
2. Take a little girl and tap her on the shoul - der,

Blue - bird, blue - bird, through my win - dow,
Take a little girl and tap her on the shoul - der,

Blue - bird, blue - bird, through my win - dow,
Take a little girl and tap her on the shoul - der,

Oh, John - ny, aren't you tired?
Oh, John - ny aren't you tired?

THIS OLD MAN

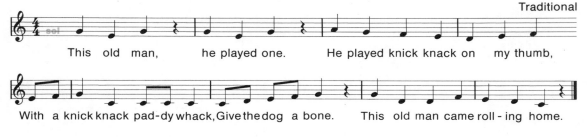

Traditional

This old man, he played one. He played knick knack on my thumb,

With a knick knack pad-dy whack, Give the dog a bone. This old man came roll - ing home.

2. two . . . on my shoe
3. three . . . on my knee
4. four . . . on my door
5. five . . . on my side
6. six . . . on my sticks

7. seven . . . up to heaven
8. eight . . . on my gate
9. nine . . . on my spine
10. ten . . . now and then (over again)

2. Teach the song, using previous rhythmic experiences (see Chart 11).
3. Use these actions with the song:

Knick knack   slap thighs twice
Paddy whack   clap hands twice

Give the dog   extend hands,
  a bone   palms up
Rolling home   hands move around
                        each other in a circle

[Note: There are many versions of "Pease Porridge Hot." This has been adapted to reinforce "sol–mi."]

INTRODUCE THE CHART

1. Ask one child to choose one line of the chart and clap the rhythm pattern.
2. Ask the class to show which pattern was clapped by holding up one, two, or three fingers. Continue with the entire chart.
3. Ask one child to sing the syllables of one line on the chart, using hand or arm signals.
4. Ask the class to identify the song. Sing the entire song; the child who identified the song leading the class.
5. Continue through the entire chart.
6. Sing the songs and use arm signals every time you hear the "sol–mi" pattern.

PEASE PORRIDGE HOT

Traditional

1. Pease   por - ridge hot,
2. Some   like   it   hot,

Pease   por - ridge cold,
some   like   it   cold,

Pease   por-ridge in the pot
Some   like   it   in the pot

nine   days   old.
nine   days   old.

4. Teach both verses of the song.
5. Play the traditional game.

Formation: Sit facing a partner

Pease	slap knees with both hands
Porridge	clap own hands
Hot (cold)	clap partners hands

Repeat above actions

Pease	slap knees
Porridge	clap hands
in the	clap partners right hand with own right hand
Pot	clap hands
Nine	clap partners left hand with own left hand
Days	clap hands
Old	slap knees

ADDITIONAL ACTIVITIES

1. Walk around the room and sing each child's name with sol–mi in various patterns to fit the syllabication of the child's name. Class will echo with syllables, using arm or hand signals.
2. Use dictation with the above activity. Put the notes on the staff, using the chalk board or individual charts. For example,

Teacher	Class sings with arm signals and writes the notes
David MacIntosh	
❘ ❘ ⊓ ❘	❘ ❘ ⊓ ❘
s m s s m	s m s s m

[Note: Putting the two eighth notes close together will show the concept of ti–ti (⊓).]

3. Proceed to Chart 25.

What Do You Hear?

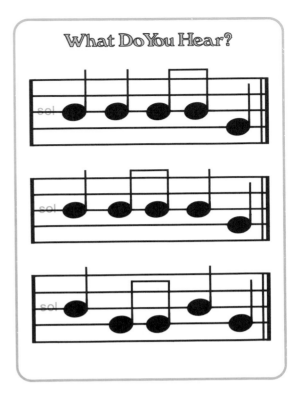

What Do You Hear?

PREPARATION FOR CHART

This chart is used for testing the children on the concept of sol–mi. This will be the first time they will have to use previous learnings, rhythms, and the position of the interval of the minor third on the staff.

INTRODUCE THE CHART

1. Clap each rhythm pattern with rhythm syllables.
2. Choose individual children to clap a line of their choice on the chart. The class will identify the pattern by holding up the correct number of fingers (1, 2, or 3).
3. Let one child sing the pattern of his choice. The class will identify the pattern. If the individual child sings the pattern correctly, the class will echo him. If he is incorrect, they remain quiet.
4. Sing one of the patterns on "loo" and have the class echo with tone syllables.
5. Use hand signals for one of the patterns without singing. The class will sing the pattern with hand signals.
6. Ask for volunteers to identify each pattern.

EVALUATION OF RHYTHMIC AND PERCEPTUAL SKILLS

Aural and Visual Acuity and Perception

1. Can the children identify a minor third on the musical staff?
2. Can they recognize long and short sounds by their rhythm pattern on the musical staff?
3. Can they sing melodic patterns using the minor third?
4. Can they read a melodic phrase on the musical staff?

A New Note–La

La

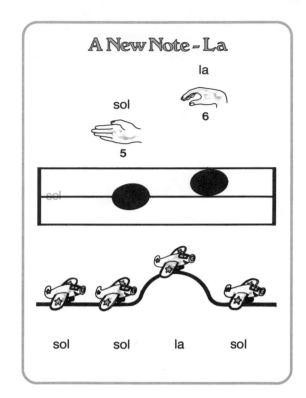

A New Note–La

sol   la

5   6

sol   sol   la   sol

[Note: Charts 26 and 27 introduce the note "la." The Evaluation for these charts appears after Chart 27.]

PREPARATION FOR THE CHART

The major second (sol–la) and the perfect fourth (mi–la) intervals are used in many playground chants and children garmes. For example,

"Johnny has a sweetheart"
"I'm bigger than you are"
"Rain, rain go away"

INTRODUCE THE CHART

1. Tell the class they are going to learn a new note that is called "la." Demonstrate the la with arm signals while singing the note. The interval can be played on the bells, piano, or recorder (G to A).

[Note: Pull the la up from the sol position and tell the children that la wants to go back to sol. This is the nature of the interval, and also it keeps the two notes in relationship to the distance of the notes on the staff.]

2. Sing sol–la with arm signals. Class echoes with arm signals. Dramatize the interval by pulling up from sol to la.
3. Ask the more mature children to explain the numerals 5 and 6 on the chart. (If necessary, review the horizontal and vertical scales in Chart 18.)

[Note: The descending minor third (sol–mi) will be represented by the numerals 5 to 3 on the numerical scale. The major second (sol–la) will be represented by 5 to 6, and the perfect fourth (la–mi), by 6 to 3. This is an extremely simplified explanation, but it will prove invaluable to the child with musical talent, even though it is a rote experience.]

4. Tap out various rhythm patterns on the chart indicating the position of sol–la. Sing the patterns with hand or arm signals:

      | ⊓ | | | | ⊓ |
      s | | s | | s | | s

5. Choose one child to lead the above activity.
6. Sing the pattern at the bottom of the chart, dramatizing with body motions and arm signals the interval of the major second (sol–la).
7. Proceed to Chart 27.

Where Is La?

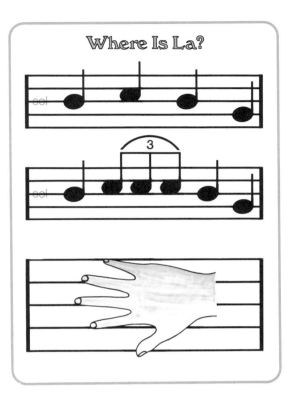
Where Is La?

4. Sing the chant, clap the rhythm pattern, and step the beat. How many times did they clap for the second beat? Let the children discover there were three claps to one beat.

   [Note: This will be an introduction to the triplet (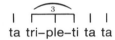), which will be used on succeeding charts. The rhythm syllables for the triplet is triple–ti. Tell the children to say triple–ti on one beat.]

5. Clap the pattern of the second line on the chart with rhythm syllables:

   ta tri–ple–ti ta ta

6. Ask one child to sing the second line with tone syllables and hand singing.
7. Place your hand over the hand on the chart. Grasp one finger and sing on one note "sol is here, where is la?"

Choose one child to come up and show where la is and sing "la is here."

8. Change the pitch and position of sol to a space and repeat the above activity.
9. Using these same activities, include the syllable "mi" (perfect fourth).

INTRODUCE THE CHART

1. Sing the first line of the chart, using hand or arm signals and body motions to show the intervals.
2. Before you introduce the second line of the chart, ask the children if they have ever said, "I'm bigger than you are" to someone on the playground. Choose several children to demonstrate how they would say it.
3. When one child has chanted:

   "I'm bigger than you are"

   s   m   m   l   s   m

   have the class echo and clap the rhythm pattern.

OTHER SONGS TO USE

"A-tisket, A-tasket"

s   s   m l   s   m m   s s   m l   s   m

"Tideo"

m   s s   l   m   s s

"French Cathedrals"

s l   m   s l   m

57

ADDITIONAL ACTIVITIES

1. Use echo clapping with the triplet:

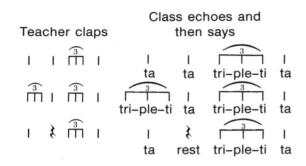

2. Make flash cards of rhythm patterns using the triplet. Move around the room so that each child will have an opportunity to clap a pattern. This can be an exciting activity if you can move from child to child without losing the beat.

3. Use echo clapping mirror image with the triplet:

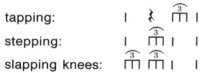

tapping:

stepping:

slapping knees:

4. Establish the pitch for sol. Make hand signals of various patterns using sol–la–mi without singing. Class echoes, singing the pattern with hand signals:

Teacher

Class sings

s	l	s s	m

5. Make flash cards of various patterns using sol–la–mi. Let the class or individuals sing the pattern, using hand signals.

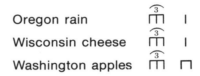

6. Find the names of states that have a triplet pattern and create a descriptive phrase. Write the pattern:

Oregon rain

Wisconsin cheese

Washington apples

[Note: This activity can be used with many words or titles. Let the children discover how many triplet words they can find in the classroom, either objects or classmate's names.]

7. Use a pattern with triplets as an ostinato to a familiar song, either clapping, tapping, or with instruments. For example, with "Are you Sleeping?" use:

EVALUATION OF RHYTHMIC AND PERCEPTUAL SKILLS

[Note: These activities require an ever-increasing amount of perception and concentration on the part of the child. Many of the activities will need repitition, though not necessarily on the same day or lesson. The more complex and integrated the activities, the more they should be performed with various familiar songs, combining previous rhythmic and melodic experiences.]

Psychomotor Development and Perception

1. Can the children move freely, feeling the beat while they sing a song?
2. Can they maintain a rhythmic ostinato using triplets while singing a song?

Aural Acuity and Perception

1. Can the children read and sing the interval of the major second and perfect fourth?
2. Can the children clap the triplet pattern while keeping the beat?

Visual Acuity and Perception

1. Can the children recognize the intervals of the major second (sol–la) and perfect fourth (la–mi) on the staff?
2. Can they write the intervals on the staff, using the correct lines or spaces for sol, la, and mi?

Camptown Races

Stephen Foster

1. Camp-town la-dies sing this song,
2. came down there with my hat caved in,

Doo - dah!   Doo - dah!
Doo - dah!   Doo - dah!

Camp-town race-track five miles long,
Went back home with a pocket full of tin,

Oh,   Doo - dah - day!
Oh,   Doo - dah - day!

Chorus

Goin' to run all night,

Goin' to run all day!   I'll

bet my money on a bob tail nag,

Some bod - y bet on the bay.

[Note: Charts 28, 29, and 30 teach and reinforce the same basic learning experience. Therefore, the Evaluation is presented at the end of Chart 30.]

PREPARATION FOR THE CHART

[Note: There are many verses to this famous song which can be found in folk song books.]

1. Teach the song.
2. Sing the song and use previous rhythm experiences (see Chart 11).

3. You may wish to introduce your class to the music of Stephen Foster through recordings.

INTRODUCE THE CHART

1. Ask one child to clap the rhythm pattern with rhythm syllables.
2. Ask another child to sing the tone syllables of the first line with hand or arm signals. The class will clap and sing the next line (Doo-dah).
3. Ask for a volunteer to sing the next line with hand or arm signals; everyone sings the last line.
4. Sing the entire chart with hand or arm signals, but put the "Doo-dah's" (second and fourth lines) inside (inner hearing).

5. Sing the first and third line of the chart with arm signals and follow the directions on the chart for "Doo-dah!" (clap and step).
6. Choose one child to sing the syllables with hand signals, having the class sing the "Doo-dah's," being careful not to lose the beat. The entire class sings the chorus.
7. Sing the song with words and arm signals.
8. If the class has learned other verses to the song, let individual children sing the first and third phrases with words and hand signals; the class sings the "Doo-dah's." All join in on the chorus.

OTHER SONGS TO USE

Put song fragments using sol–la–mi on the chalkboard or on a large chart for future use. Sing or use rhythm activities for those portions of the song where the tone syllables are unfamiliar:

ADDITIONAL ACTIVITIES

1. Sing the song, making large arm movements for each phrase:

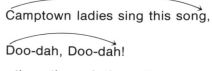

Continue through the entire song.
2. On a large piece of paper or on the chalkboard, draw a picture of the melody line. For example,

phrase 1: ⌒
phrase 2: ∖ ∖

Continue through the entire song.
3. Have the class decide which phrases are the same and which are different. Use geometric shapes or letters. For example,

phrase 1: ○
phrase 2: △
phrase 3: ○
phrase 4: □

Encourage the children to discover similarities and differences of other familiar songs. This activity will be invaluable to them when they begin the study of form in music.
4. Proceed to the next chart.

Mystery Songs

1. TIDEO

U.S. Singing Game

Pass one win-dow, Ti - de - o,

pass two win-dows, Ti - de - o,

Pass three win-dows, Ti - de - o,

Jin-gle at the win-dow, Ti - de - o.

Chorus

Ti - de - o,   Ti - de - o,

Jin-gle at the win-dow, Ti - de - o.

PREPARATION FOR THE CHART

As a general preparation, sing various patterns using sol–la–mi with hand or arm signals and echo singing. Establish the pitch for sol:

Teacher	Class
l ⊓ l l	l ⊓ l l
s ll s m	s ll s m
⊓ l ⊓ l	⊓ l ⊓ l
ll s ll s	ll s ll s

For the more mature children, begin some of the patterns on mi:

l l ⊓ l	l l ⊓ l
m s l s m	m s l s m
l ⊓ l l	l ⊓ l l
m l s m m	m l s m m

Tideo

1. Teach the song.
2. Sing the song and use previous rhythmic experiences (Chart 11). Encourage free relaxed movements.
3. Walk the beat and sing only the first word of each measure (accent):

    Pass – – – Ti – – –
    Pass – – – Ti – – –
    Pass – – – Ti – – – etc.

French Cathedrals

1. Teach the song. Be aware of the B flat (♭) in the third measure.
2. Sing the song and step the beat. How many beats do you feel (2)?
3. Sing the song and sway back and forth to the beat (like a big bell).

2. FRENCH CATHEDRALS

Or - le - ans, Beau - gen - cy,
ohr - leh - awns, boh - zhan - see,

No - tre Dam - e de Cler - y, Ven-
noh - truh - da - muh, duh - kleh - ry, vahn-

dom - e, Ven - dom - e.
doh - muh, vahn - doh - muh.

Hey, Ho! Nobody Home

1. Teach the song.
2. Sing the song and use previous rhythmic experiences.

[Note: Teach the dotted quarter note and single eighth note by rote (♩. ♪) when clapping the pattern. They will be introduced on a later chart. The rhythm syllables are ta–a and ti, respectively.]

3. HEY, HO! NOBODY HOME

English Round

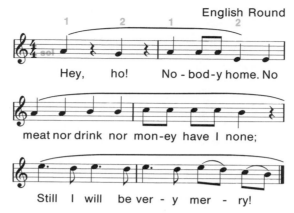

Hey, ho! No - bod-y home. No

meat nor drink nor mon-ey have I none;

Still I will be ver - y mer - ry!

INTRODUCE THE CHART

1. Choose individual children to clap the rhythm pattern of each song. Many children will be able to identify the songs by their rhythm pattern.
2. If one child identifies the song correctly, ask him to sing the phrase on the chart with hand signals.
3. Have a volunteer choose a phrase on the chart and do only the hand signals, without singing. Have the class identify the melody by holding up the correct number of fingers to correspond to the lines on the chart.

ADDITIONAL ACTIVITIES

Tideo

1. Teach the traditional singing game.

   Formation: Circle with hands joined high to form windows. One child in the center.

- Children sing the song while the child in the center goes in and out the windows.
- On the fourth phrase the child chooses the next person to be in the middle by stopping in front of him.
- While singing the chorus; the two children make the following motions:

Ti-	slap own knees
de-	clap own hands
o	touch fists of partner
Jingle	slap knees
at the	clap own hands
win-	partners clap right hands
dow	clap own hands
Ti-	partners clap left hands
de-	clap own hands
o	fists at the side of body

- The child who was chosen continues the game and the first child steps out of the center of the circle.

[Note: The use of the fist is to prepare the children for the "do" syllable.]

2. Sing the song and draw a picture of the melody in the air with large arm movements. This can later be put on a large piece of paper.

[Note: Each child's picture will be different. An interesting art project is to make the melodic phrases in different colors with heavy crayon and wash with water color.]

French Cathedrals

1. After the song is learned, divide the class and sing as a two-part round. Later in the year they may be able to sing the song in three parts. When the first group

comes to the end of the round, continue singing "Vendome" on la–sol–mi until the second group comes to the end. Repeat the song several times.

2. Divide the class. One group sings sol–mi or sol–la–mi with syllables or words (ding–dong or ding, ding, dong) as an ostinato while the second group sings the song. Use hand or arm signals for sol–la–mi.

3. Encourage the children to decide where the song is soft (*p*) and where it should get louder (<).

Hey, Ho! Nobody Home

1. After the song is learned, divide the class and sing as a round.
2. Create an instrumental ostinato, taking a pattern from the melody:

no-bod-y   home
ꞁ   ⊓   ꞁ   ⸯ   wood block

mon-ey have I none
⊓   ⊓   ꞁ   ⸯ   triangle or sticks

Let the children decide which instrument or sound fits the mood of the song. Have one group sing the song or sing as a round, while several ostinatos are playing the accompaniment. (Let the instruments set the beat before the singers begin.)

3. Divide the class and form two circles, one within the other. Walk the beat (two steps to the measure) as a round while singing the song. Change direction on each phrase. Group 2 stands still until it begins to sing.
4. Turn to the next chart.

What Do You Hear?

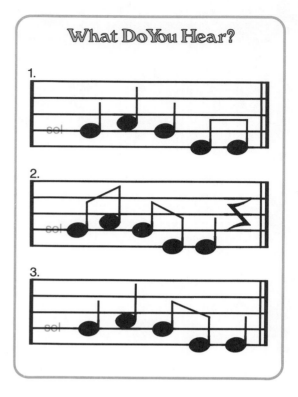

PREPARATION FOR THE CHART

This chart is used for testing the concept of sol–la (major second). The activity involves the reading of the rhythm pattern, the reading of notes on the staff, and the ability to read and sing the correct intervals. If the previous charts have been thoroughly understood, the children will experience the gratifying feeling of success at their ability to read music.

INTRODUCE THE CHART

1. Choose one child to clap the rhythm pattern of Line 1 of the chart. If he is correct, the class will echo. If he is incorrect, they will remain silent. Continue through the entire chart.

2. Review the syllable names on the chart. The children will discover that the melody is the same, only the rhythm pattern is different.

3. Sing one of the melodies on the chart, using tone syllables and hand signals. Tell the children to raise one finger if they heard melody one, two fingers if it was melody two, and so on. Ask for a volunteer to sing one of the melodies for the class to identify.

4. Choose any one of the melodies on the chart. Make the hand signals, but do not sing. Can the children identify the melody?

5. Sing one of the melodies on a neutral syllable ("loo"). Let the class echo you with tone syllables and hand signals.

EVALUATION OF RHYTHMIC AND PERCEPTUAL SKILLS

Psychomotor Development

1. Can the children sing a song and maintain a rhythmic, vocal, or instrumental ostinato?

2. Can they move freely with increased coordination and body awareness?
   Can they differentiate four beats and two beats through body motions?

Aural and Visual Acuity

1. Can the children sing a major second while reading the interval on the staff?

2. Can they recognize the major second (sol–la) on the musical staff?

Bobwhite

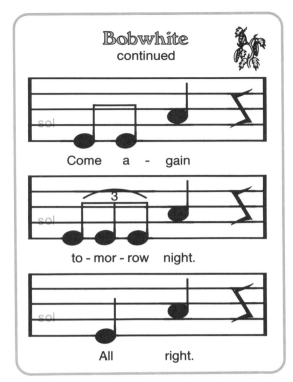

PREPARATION FOR THE CHART

1. Sing various patterns with hand singing using sol–la–mi. Children will echo:

    | ⊓ | |
    s ll s m

    | ⊓ | |
    l s s m s

2. Tell the children to listen carefully with inner hearing while you make the hand signals for the first two measures of "French Cathedrals":

    ⊓ | ⊓ |
    s l m s l m

Can the children identify the song? Sing the first two measures with the children, using hand signals.

3. Repeat this activity with "Ring Around the Rosey":

    ⊓ ⊓ | |
    s s m l s m

[Note: When you come to the interval of the perfect fourth (mi–la or, inverted, la–mi), stop and repeat the interval. Tell the children they are singing a perfect fourth. Refer to the vertical scale and let them count down from la to mi or up from mi to la.]

4. Make hand signals for mi–la or la–mi

without singing. Ask the children to listen to the sound they hear inside. Ask them to sing the interval with hand signals. (If they are insecure, start the pattern on sol: sol–la–mi.)

5. Sing mi–la–mi–la with hand signals. Class echoes. Sing various rhythm patterns with la–mi or mi–la for the class to echo.

6. *Two-hand singing.* This activity should be used many times during the school year. Divide the class into two groups. Tell one group to follow and sing the tone signals of your left hand, and the other group to follow your right hand. Establish the pitch on a unison "sol," and then proceed to two parts, one hand at a time. Begin this activity slowly and keep the patterns sim-

ple, frequently returning to a unison note. (This will check the tonality.) For example, have one group sing "sol" and the other group sing "sol–la–sol–mi–mi":

R.H. s l s m m – – – – –
L.H. s – – – – s l s m m

The "mi" is held as long as you hold the hand signal. See page 84 for photo of two-hand singing.

INTRODUCE THE CHART

1. Read the words with the class. (Keep the beat while moving from chart to chart.) Tell the children that the bobwhite is a small bird usually found in the midwest and eastern states. Children in the west will be more familiar with the quail, which is a relative of the bobwhite. The bobwhite's call is a clear whistle that is a perfect fourth (mi–la) and sounds like "bob–white."
2. Read and clap the rhythm pattern of both charts. Ask the children how many syllables the word "tomorrow" has. How many times do they have to clap? (3) Do they remember what to say for the triplet? (triple–ti) Be sure they make the rest motion and keep the beat.

   [Note: This will be the introduction to three beats on a chart. All previous rhythmic experiences have been in duple time, two and four.]

3. Say the words and step the beat. How many beats do they feel? (3)

   [Note: When stepping triple beats, it is sometimes helpful to say, "Step–tiptoe." This will emphasize the accent on the first beat and also provide an introduction to the waltz without calling it "dancing."]

4. Establish the pitch for sol. Ask the children if they can sing "la," then sing "mi." Repeat this interval several times.
5. Sing the entire exercise, using hand or arm signals and tone syllables.
6. Sing the song with words and hand signals.
7. Divide the class into two groups. First group sings the question, second group sings the answer with hand signals.
8. Choose two children to sing the question and answer.

ADDITIONAL ACTIVITIES

1. The children should be encouraged to write music. This will combine listening, writing, reading, and singing activities to further develop and reinforce new learnings:

   | Teacher claps: | | |
   Children echo: |
   All clap and say: ta – ta –   ta ti–ti ta –
   Children write:

   Put the pattern on the chalkboard.

2. *Dictation for "Hey, Ho Nobody Home."* Draw a staff on the chalkboard and place "sol" on the second line:

   [Note: If the children have individual music staves with cut-out notes and rests, it will be invaluable in the teaching of melodic skills.]

   Tell the children the first note above sol is la. Ask one child to show the correct position for la on the staff:

Sing "la" and make the rest motion, then sing "sol" and make the rest motion. What comes after la? (𝄽) Ask for a volunteer to add the rest. What comes after the rest? (sol) Have volunteers add sol, and then another rest. Continue with the rest of the melodic pattern:

What is the name of the song? Sing what the children have written. The class will be delighted to find they have written the first phrase of "Hey, Ho! Nobody Home." Sing the song with la–sol as an ostinato.

3. The last activity can be used many times with song fragments to reinforce a particular interval or rhythm pattern.

EVALUATION OF RHYTHMIC AND PERCEPTUAL SKILLS

Aural and Visual Acuity and Perception

1. Can the children hear the interval of the perfect fourth while reading a chart or observing hand signals?
2. Can they read the chart and recognize the perfect fourth?

Musical Development and Social Maturity

1. Can the children hear a melody and place the notes on the staff?
2. Are they becoming increasingly confident with musical notation?

Sol-Mi-Do

Do

Do'

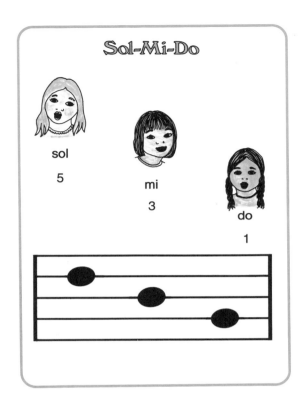

Sol-Mi-Do

sol

5

mi

3

do

1

[Note: Charts 32 and 33 combine a single lesson, and therefore the "Evaluation" is presented at the end of Chart 33.]

INTRODUCE THE CHART

1. Tell the children they have sung "do" many times, usually at the end of a song.
2. Review some familiar songs. Stop the song just before the final note (do):

   Old MacDonald—"ee–i–ee–i– (o)"
   Bingo—"and Bingo was his (name–o)"
   Twinkle, Twinkle—"how I wonder
   what you (are)"

3. The hand signal for "do" is a strongly clenched fist.

   [Note: The tone syllable "do" is the home tone or key syllable of many songs, and most children's songs are written in a major key.]

4. Sing the chart slowly, holding each syllable for four beats.

   [Note: Encourage the children to sing each note with adequate breath support. When singing "sol" and "do," tell them to make their mouths like O's. When singing "mi," have them smile with their lips pulled back and the jaws relaxed (see Chart 17).]

5. Use the hand signals on the chart and have the children sing "sol–mi–do" with arm signals.

6. Do this activity and sing "5–3–1" with arm signals. Why is "do" called "one"? Put the vertical scale on the board (Chart 17) to illustrate the position of "do."

7. Create various rhythm patterns on the chart with hand signals. Have the children echo with arm signals.

Teacher sings	Class echoes
❘ ⊓ ❘ ❘	❘ ⊓ ❘ ❘
s m m d d	s m m d d
⊓ ❘ ⊓ ❘	⊓ ❘ ⊓ ❘
d d m s s m	d d m s s m

[Note: These patterns can be as complex as the children are capable of doing. Start slowly and progress to the more difficult patterns. You will find that the children will have more success singing the descending sol–do than singing the ascending do–sol.]

8. Establish the pitch for sol. Create various rhythm patterns on the chart but *do not* sing. The class will sing the patterns you indicate with hand or arm signals:

Teacher	Class sings with signals
❘ ❘ ⊓ ❘	❘ ❘ ⊓ ❘
s m d d d	s m d d d
⊓ ❘ ⊓ ❘	⊓ ❘ ⊓ ❘
s m d s m d	s m d s m d

As the children become more confident, use a two measure pattern such as:

❘ ⊓ ❘ ❘   ❘ ⸰ ❘ ⸰
s m m d d   m   s

Ask one of the children to lead the class in this activity.

9. Point to the chart, either the syllables or notes, while the class sings and dramatizes the position of the notes on the staff. For example,

- sol stand up, with arm signals for "sol."
- mi   bend the knees or sit down with arm signals for "mi."
- do   kneel down with fists on the floor for "do."

Vary the rhythmic pattern while doing this activity.

10. Use your hand to illustrate the five lines of the staff. Establish the position of sol and have volunteers find "mi," and then "do." Vary the position of sol. Sing the intervals as they are identified.

11. Turn to the next chart.

Old Woman

American Folk Song

1. Old Wo-man, old wo-man, Are you fond of card - ing?

Old wo-man, old wo-man, Are you fond of card - ing?

Speak a lit - tle loud - er, sir! I'm ver - y hard of hear - ing.

2. Old woman, old woman,
Are you fond of spinning? *(Repeat)*
Speak a little louder sir!
I'm very hard of hearing.

3. Old woman, old woman,
Will you darn by stocking? *(Repeat)*
Speak a little louder, sir!
I'm very hard of hearing.

4. Old woman, old woman,
Will you let me court you? *(Repeat)*
Speak a little louder, sir!
I just begin to hear you.

5. Old woman, old woman,
Don't you want to marry me? *(Repeat)*
Oh, my goodness gracious me!
I think that now I hear you.

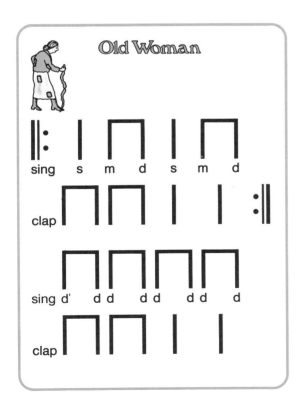

PREPARATION FOR THE CHART

1. Teach the song (all verses).
2. Sing the song, using previous rhythmic experiences (Chart 11).

INTRODUCE THE CHART

1. Choose one child to clap the rhythm pattern on the chart with rhythm syllables. Be certain to observe the repeat signs.
2. Choose another child to sing the first line of the chart with hand or arm signals. The class will tap the second line.
3. Read and sing the entire chart with tone syllables, arm signals, tapping, and clapping.

4. Use flash cards for inner hearing with the chart:

feel   step   instruments

Choose individuals to sing Lines 1 and 3 and have the class follow the directions on the flash cards for Lines 2 and 4.

5. Sing the song with words and hand signals.
6. After the class has learned all the verses, divide them into two groups—one to sing the questions (first two lines) and the other to sing the part of the "old woman." Use hand signals and rhythmic activities. Ask two children to perform the part of the "old woman" and the question.

69

ADDITIONAL ACTIVITIES

1. *Similarities and Differences.* Which phrases are alike? Make a picture of the melody, first in the air with arm movements, then on paper:

Phrase 1:   Phrase 2:   Phrase 3:

The form can also be shown with letters or shapes:

A A B   or   ○ ○ △

2. *Instruments.* Read and play the pattern on the chart with rhythm instruments:

   Lines 1 and 2—woodblock or sticks
   Lines 3 and 4—tambourine or drum

Pass out the C–E–G and high C resonator bells. Let the children discover which bells will play the melody.

"Old woman" G–E–C
"Speak a little louder, etc." C'–C–C–C

This activity can also be performed on the recorder, song flute, or song bells.

[Note: The notes C–E–C–C' will be closest to a child's vocal range.]

EVALUATION OF RHYTHMIC AND PERCEPTUAL SKILLS

Aural Acuity and Perception

1. Can the children hear and sing the descending major third (mi–do)?

2. Can they hear the similarities and differences in a melody?
3. Can they recognize the high do (do')?

Visual Acuity and Perception

1. Can the children recognize the "do" on the musical staff?
2. Can they read the pattern on the chart while singing or playing an instrument?

Musical Development and Social Maturity

Can the children successfully relate previous musical learnings to a familiar song?

Mystery Songs

American Singing Game

1. We're go-ing 'round the mount-ain,

two by two, We're go-ing 'round the

mount-ain, two by two, We're

go -ing 'round the mount-ain, two by

two, So rise, Sal-ly, rise.

2. Let's see you make a motion, two by two, (3x)
   So rise, Sally, rise.

3. That's a mighty fine motion, two by two, (3x)
   So rise, Sally, rise.

4. Let's see you make another, two by two, (3x)
   So rise, Sally, rise.

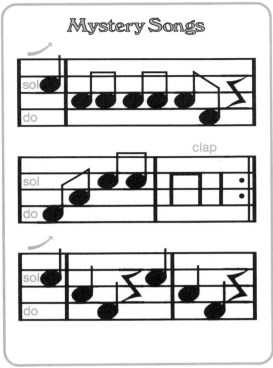

[Note: The Evaluation for Charts 34 and 35 is combined and appears at the end of Chart 35.]

PREPARATION FOR THE CHART

We're Going 'Round the Mountain

[Note: the rhythm pattern of this familiar folk song has been adapted to previous learning experiences. (review "an anacrusis" on Chart 8).]

1. Teach the song (all verses).
2. Sing the song and use previous rhythmic experiences.
3. Teach the singing game.

   Formation: Circle with partners.
   • Verse 1—Partners join hands and walk the beat around the circle. The beat will be either four steps or two steps to the measure, depending on the maturity of your class and the tempo of the song.
   • Verse 2—Swing your partner. This may be done by linking elbows or holding hands. Walk the beat. You may wish to change direction on each phrase.
   • Verse 3—Mirror image. (This will allow for many variations.) At the end of Verse 2, sing a child's name, "So rise, Johnny, rise." Johnny will make a motion. For example, snap fingers, hold a grotesque pose (balance), etc. The class will mirror the motion of Johnny.
   • Verse 4—Repeat Verse 3 and call on another child to make "a mighty fine motion."

4. Sing the song and create a rhythmic ostinato, such as: slap knees, clap, snap, snap. (Begin the ostinato on the first beat, not the anacrusis.)

Love Somebody

1. Teach the song. There are many verses to this song (not given here).
2. Sing the song and use previous rhythmic experiences.

    Sing measure 1 with arm signals—clap measure 2

    Sing measure 3 with arm signals—step measure 4

    Sing measure 5 with arm signals—feel measure 6

    Sing and step the rhythm pattern for measures 7–8

[Note: The children will notice the six-teenth notes by having to make four quick steps to the beat. (The sixteenth note was introduced on Chart 19.) If the children wish to know the rhythm sylla-bles for the sixteenth-note pattern, tell them to say ti–di–ti–di on one beat. The sixteenth note will be developed further on succeeding charts.]

Roll Over

1. Teach the song, singing all ten verses, from "ten in the bed" through "one in the bed."

[Note: Remember that repetition offers an opportunity to the insecure or nonpartic-ipating child who often is listening and waiting to become a part of the song. A song such as "Roll Over" will give him the time and the opportunity to develop a positive attitude toward himself in rela-tionship to music.]

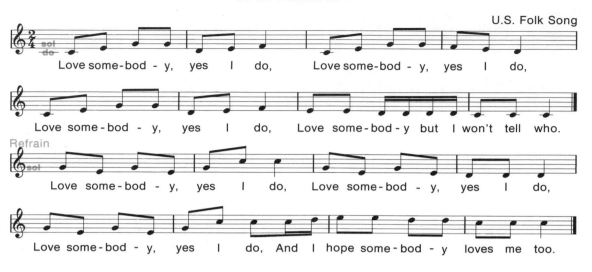

LOVE SOMEBODY

U.S. Folk Song

Love some-bod - y, yes I do, Love some-bod - y, yes I do,

Love some-bod - y, yes I do, Love some-bod-y but I won't tell who.

Refrain

Love some-bod - y, yes I do, Love some-bod - y, yes I do,

Love some-bod - y, yes I do, And I hope some-bod - y loves me too.

ROLL OVER

Traditional

1. There were ten in the bed and the lit-tle one said, "Roll o - ver, Roll
2. There were nine . . .

o - ver," So they all rolled o - ver and one fell out. There was

one in the bed so the lit - tle one said, "Good night, Good night."

2. Sing the song and use previous rhythmic experiences. Be aware of the anacrusis.
3. Choose ten children and number them from ten to one. Have the entire class sing the song while clapping the pattern. Each numbered child will sing "Roll over" using the arm signals for sol–mi–do. The last child (number one) will sing "Good night" on mi–do.
4. Sing the song, clap the pattern, and use arm signals for "Roll over" (sol–mi–do) and "Good night" (mi–do).

INTRODUCE THE CHART

1. Ask a volunteer to choose one line on the chart and clap the rhythm pattern. Can the class identify the pattern by holding up one, two, or three fingers?
2. Ask for volunteers to sing a line of the chart with hand signals. Can the class identify the song? Sing the entire song.
3. Continue through the entire chart. The child who correctly identifies the song may lead the class while they sing.

OTHER SONGS TO USE

"Skip To My Lou"

| ❙ | ❙ | ❙ | ❙ | ❙ | ⊓ | ❙ | ᘏ |
| m | m | d | d | m | m | m | s |

"Paw Paw Patch"

| ❙ | ❙ | ❙ | ❙ | ❙ | ⊓ | ❙ | ❙ |
| d | d | d | d | m | s | s | m | d |

"Down Came a Lady"

| ❙ | ❙ | ❙ | ❙ | ❙ | ❙ | ❙ | ᘏ |
| d | d | m | m | d | d | s |

ADDITIONAL ACTIVITIES

1. Make up individual charts to use for dictation. Establish the position for sol or "do" (3rd line, fourth space, etc.):

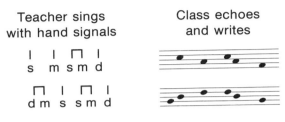

Teacher sings with hand signals

| ❙ | ❙ | ⊓ | ❙ |
| s | m | s m | d |

| ⊓ | ❙ | ⊓ | ❙ |
| d m | s | s m | d |

Class echoes and writes

2. Establish the pitch for sol. Make the hand signals for a melodic pattern using sol–mi–do but *do not* sing. The class will sing the tone syllables with hand signals.
3. Make flash cards of various melodic patterns using sol–mi–do:

| ❙ ᘏ ⊓ ❙ | ⊓ ❙ ⊓ ❙ | ❙ ⊓ ⊓ ❙ |
| s   m m d | d m s m m d | s m m s s d |

Establish the pitch for sol and hold up a flash card. The class will sing the pattern with hand signals.

[*Note: When the children are confident with this activity, ask individuals to sing the flash cards. Let each child establish his or her own pitch. This will vary with each child.*]

4. Turn to Chart 35.

The Triad

PREPARATION FOR THE CHART

A chord is formed by sounding groups of tones simultaneously. A **triad** is a chord formed by sounding three tones simultaneously.

[Note: A discussion of prefixes will clarify the concept of the triad:

tri—tricycle (three wheels)
triangle (three sided figure)
triad (three tones)]

The *tonic* chord is a triad using sol–mi–do and is most commonly heard in western music. Most songs begin and end on one of the tones of the tonic chord. The tonic chord is often called the key chord, because it is built on "do," which establishes the key in which a song is to be performed.

INTRODUCE THE CHART

1. Divide the class into three groups, and establish the pitch for sol.

   - The entire class sings "sol."
   - Group 1 sings "sol" and continues to sing with good breath support, taking a breath whenever necessary.
   - Give the hand signal for "mi." Groups 2 and 3 sing "mi."
   - Group 1 continues singing "sol," Group 2 continues singing "mi."
   - Give the hand signal for "do" to Group 3.

2. Tell the children they are singing a chord. Do the above activity several times. When the children hear the chord for the first time, they are amazed.

   [Note: The tendency will be to oversing (shout) at first. Encourage the children to sing the chord softly, with a beautiful tone—jaws relaxed and lips formed properly for each syllable (see Chart 35).]

3. Divide the class into three groups. Build the triad on "loo," starting with sol, then mi, and finally "do." Start the triad softly and gradually get louder (<). You will find that many children will alter the pitch upward as they get louder. Begin the crescendo gradually. If the pitch begins to change, decrescendo (>) until the children can hear the chord.

4. For the more mature children, build the chord on "loo" and when the pitch is established, give a signal (clap, tap the desk, etc.) to stop the singing. At a given signal, sing the chord again. Repeat this activity several times.

The Triad

Sing
and
Listen

EVALUATION OF RHYTHMIC AND PERCEPTUAL SKILLS

Aural Acuity and Perception

1. Can the children hear the descending thirds that are used in a triad?
2. Can they hear and reproduce a major chord?
3. Can they recognize the triad within a familiar song?

Visual Acuity and Perception

1. Can the children recognize the "sol–mi–do" on the musical staff?
2. Can they establish the position of sol–mi–do on individual charts?

Question and Answer

[Note: This chart is a preparation for creative activities involving rhythm and melody. This may sound highly technical to the classroom teacher with little training in music, but children who have performed the previous rhythmic and melodic activities will thoroughly enjoy composing their own patterns. You will find that children have a tendency to echo the pattern they have just heard, but encourage them to create their own pattern. They will soon surprise you.]

PREPARATION FOR THE CHART

1. Creative Rhythmic Activity. Tell the children they will be composing their own rhythm pattern after the class echoes the teacher. Choose individual children to create a pattern.

Teacher claps	Class echoes	One child claps
| | ⊓ |	| | ⊓ |	⊓ ⊓ | |
⊓ | ⊓ |	⊓ | ⊓ |	| ⧵ ⊓ |

Put a pattern on the board, your own or one of the children's:

Teacher claps A
(A) \| \| ⊓ \|

One child claps B
(B) ⊓ \| ⊓ \|

Teacher and class clap A
(A) \| \| ⊓ \|

One child claps C, etc.
(C) \| ⧵ ⊓ \|

Move around the room so each child has a turn to create his own pattern, keeping the beat. (The above activity will prepare the children for **rondo** form: A B A C A.)

2. Creative Melodic Activity:

Teacher sings
with arm
signals   Class echoes   One child sings

| \| \| \| \| | \| \| \| \| | \| \| \| \| |
| s s s m | s s s m | s m s m |

| \| ⊓ \| \| | \| ⊓ \| \| | \| ⊓ \| \| |
| s l l s m | s l l s m | s m m d d |

Teacher moves from child to child, asking a musical question with arm signals. Child answers with arm signals. If the question has four beats, the answer will have four beats:

Teacher	Child
| | | ⧵	| | | ⧵
d m s	s m d
How are you?	I am fine.
⊓ ⊓ | |	| | | ⧵
s s l l s m	s l s
Do you have a pen-cil?	Yes, I do.

[Note: The answer will not always end on "do" (home tone), but as the children

become more confident, they will create longer patterns and use different melodic combinations.]

INTRODUCE THE CHART

1. Clap the rhythm pattern of the first line with rhythm syllables. How many beats does each measure have? (2)
2. Ask one child to clap the rhythm pattern of the second line. What happens to the last beat? Tell the child he can clap any pattern he wishes to complete the phrase. What will it be? (⧵, \|, ⊓, ⊓̅³̅)
3. Ask the class to clap the second line, using the "original" rhythm pattern.
4. Continue through the chart, letting one child create the final beat.

75

5. Establish the pitch for "do." Sing the first line of the chart with the class, using hand signals.
6. Divide the class. One group sings the question, the other group sings the answer.
7. Choose two children to sing the question and answer, using hand signals.
8. Put the second line of the chart on the board. Sing the first measure with the class. Choose one child to sing the answer, using any syllable he wishes, with the correct hand signal. Put the tone symbol on the chalkboard under the rhythm symbol.
9. Continue throughout the entire chart, creating an "original" melodic pattern.
10. Divide the class. One group sings the question, the other sings the answer, using the "original" rhythmic and melodic pattern.
11. Ask two children to sing the entire chart with hand signals and tone syllables.
12. To encourage the creative child, ask for volunteers to create a different ending for each phrase. Class sings the question and one child sings the answer, creating his own melody.

ADDITIONAL ACTIVITIES

1. Make up words to the conversation. For example,

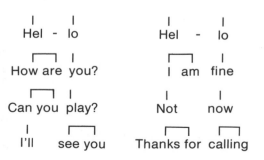

2. Create another conversation using four beats to a measure. Use the syllables sol–mi–do at first, later, add the la.

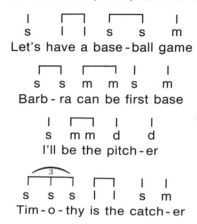

EVALUATION OF RHYTHMIC AND PERCEPTUAL SKILLS

Aural and Visual Acuity and Perception

1. Can the children read and hear the perfect fifth? (sol–do, do–sol)
2. Can they read the musical symbols on the chart and sing the melodic phrase?
3. Can the children recognize the perfect fifth?

Musical Development and Social Maturity

1. Can the children fit the syllabication of a word to a rhythm pattern?
2. Can they create musical conversations in two-measure or four-measure phrases?
3. Can they concentrate on longer rhythmic and melodic phrases?

4. Are more children volunteering to create a rhythmic or melodic pattern?
5. Can the children create original rhythmic and melodic patterns?
6. Can they perform their original patterns with confidence?

Surprise Symphony

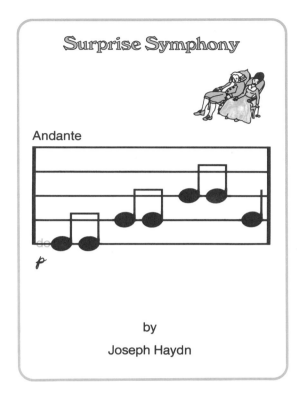

[Note: In order to use this chart you will need to play a recording of Haydn's Surprise Symphony. This can be obtained through your Music Department. Review Chart 19. If you wish to tell the class more about Joseph Haydn, Lillian Baldwin's Music for Young Listeners, Blue Book (Silver Burdett) is invaluable.]

PREPARATION FOR THE CHART

1. Recall the story of "Papa" Haydn.
2. Joseph Haydn's orchestra often played for guests after dinner. The ladies would come to the concert in their powdered wigs and hooped skirts and the gentlemen in their knee breeches and buckled shoes. Perhaps they ate too much dinner, or they didn't know how to listen to good music, so they would often sleep through the concert. This is what made Haydn decide to play a joke.

   Andante (ahn-dahn-tā) means moderately slow, just right for someone to take a little nap. This is where Haydn decided to surprise everyone. The music starts softly and gently, and just when Haydn figured everyone would be nodding, every instrument in the orchestra plays as loudly as it can—just one note that makes a chord. (Remember the chord? Several notes played or sung at the same time.)

   "There," said Haydn, with a twinkle in his eye. "That should wake them up." He was not mistaken. Even though there were no more loud chords, everyone wanted to stay awake, just in case.
3. Play the recording of the "Andante" to the *Surprise Symphony*. Can the class tell why this composition is called the *Surprise Symphony*?

[Note: You may wish to play more of the record, depending on the attention span of your class.]

1. Ask the children to read the music on the chart and hear the melody in their heads. Use hand signals.
2. Establish the pitch for "do." Ask the children to sing the chart with hand signals.
3. Ask the class where they have heard this melody before. Who is the composer?
4. Play the record again. Ask the children to raise their hands or make the hand signals every time they hear the theme (d d m m s s m).
5. Ask the children if the melody on the recording is *always* exactly the same.

   • Can they recognize the theme when there is another melody playing at the same time?
   • Can they recognize the theme when the rhythm pattern changes?

d d d d m m m m s s s s m m m m

6. Is the theme always played softly (*p*)?

1. Encourage the children to do further research on the life and times of Joseph Haydn:

   • type of dress
   • housing—castles and palaces
   • kings and queens
   • compare the life of George Washington and Joseph Haydn.

2. Tell the children that the minuet was a popular dance of the period, which they might like to perform.

Aural Acuity and Perception

Are the children able to listen to a composition and discover similarities and differences?

• recurring themes?
• melody played higher and lower?
• alteration in rhythm pattern?

Musical Development

Are the children demonstrating an increasing enjoyment while listening to a composition?

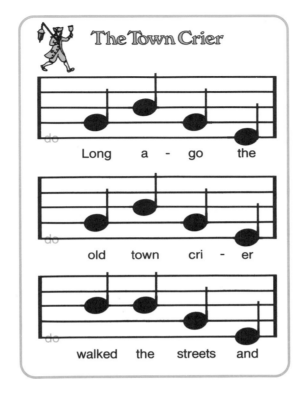

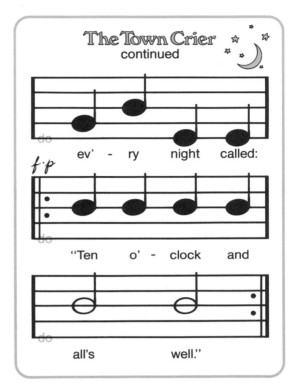

PREPARATION FOR THE CHART

Tell the children that before we had radio, telephone, television, newspapers, and electric clocks the villages had town criers. These were men that walked through the town, ringing a large bell and told everyone the news and the time of the day or night by calling out at intervals. The town crier found that when he sang the time, his voice carried further and sounded more interesting. The bell would help him keep the beat as he walked and it announced to everyone that he was coming.

INTRODUCE THE CHART

1. Read the chart with hand or arm signals and put the melody inside. On what tone syllable does the song begin? (mi) (Move from one chart to the other without losing the beat.)

2. Step the beat and make the arm signals. How many steps did they take on the last measure? (4) How many times did they clap on the last measure? (2)

3. Tell the children the last two notes are half-notes. Each note gets two beats and the rhythm syllables are ta–a, ta–a.

4. Ask one child to establish the pitch for sol. (This will be a relative pitch.) Ask another child to sing "mi." This is the starting tone.

5. Establish the beat. (Say, "one, two, ready, sing."
   - Step the beat
   - Sing the chart with tone syllables and hand signals
   - Observe the repeat signs (‖: :‖).

6. Ask the children what the *f* and *p* means on the last phrase. (Sing the last phrase loud—*f*; sing the repeat softly—*p*.) Tell the

79

children the "town crier" is walking away and his voice is getting softer.

7. Read the words with the class.

- Sing the chart with words and hand signals
- Step the beat
- Observe the dynamics ($f \cdot p$)
- Observe the repeat signs (||: :||)

ADDITIONAL ACTIVITIES

1. Divide the class. Group 1 steps the rhythm pattern (l l l l), and Group 2 steps only the half-notes (♩ ♩).
2. Using the same activity, have Group 1 sing the song with words and hand signals, while Group 2 sings "ding–dong" on sol–do, throughout the entire song.
3. Form two circles, one within the other. The outer circle walks the beat while singing the song. The inner circle walks the half-notes, singing "ding–dong" on sol–do.
4. Draw three lines on the floor about a foot apart (sol–mi–do). Choose one child to step the melody while the class sings the song.

sol
mi
do
etc.

[Note: This activity will provide a welcome break in the day when the children are restless or need a change of pace.]

5. Pass out the resonator bells to form a major triad. For example,

    C E G,   F A C,   G B D

[Note: Other triads will need a sharp (♯) or flat (♭).]

Let the children create an ostinato while the class sings the song. Let them try playing a major triad on the first beat of each measure. Later, let them create a rhythm pattern to play on the bells.

EVALUATION OF RHYTHMIC AND PERCEPTUAL SKILLS

[Note: The preceding charts emphasized the importance of the tone syllable "do." In Western music and in many children's songs, the "do" is often the final note, giving a feeling of finality at the end of the song.]

Psychomotor Development and Perception

Are the children becoming increasingly confident while performing rhythmic activities?

- Walking or stepping the beat in a relaxed manner
- Combining integrated activities

Aural Acuity and Perception

1. Can the children read and hear the interval of the perfect fifth (sol–do, do–sol) and major third (mi–do, do–mi)?
2. Can they differentiate notes of varying lengths (l, ⊓, ♩)?
   Are they becoming increasingly aware of various intervals (sol–la, sol–mi, la–sol, la–mi)?

Visual Acuity and Perception

1. Can the children read a chart and perform the activities, from simple to complex?
   - Read the pattern
   - Sing the syllables
   - Observe repeat signs :||
   - Observe dynamic markings ($f \cdot p$)
2. Can they recognize and perform various intervals on the chart?

A New Note–Re

Re

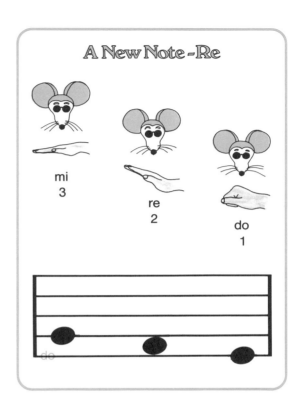

[Note: The next four charts (39–42) teach the major second interval. The Evaluation for these charts appears at the end of Lesson 42.]

PREPARATION FOR THE CHART

1. Teach the song.
2. Clap the rhythm pattern of the song as a mystery song. Although the time signature is in 6/8, clap the pattern with the beat in two:

♩.   ♩.   ♫♫   ♫♫
1   2   1   2

3. Sing the song and step or walk the beat.
4. Sing the song and use previous rhythmic experiences (see Chart 11). Use flash cards for inner hearing.

THREE BLIND MICE

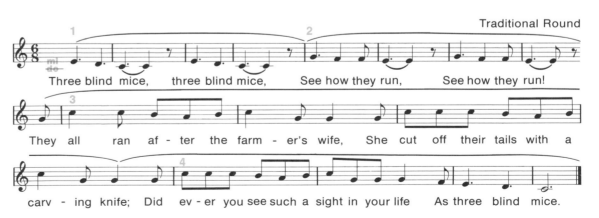

Traditional Round

Three blind mice,   three blind mice,   See how they run,   See how they run!

They all   ran af - ter the farm - er's wife,   She cut off their tails with a

carv - ing knife; Did ev - er you see such a sight in your life   As three blind mice.

[Note: The notation on the chart differs from the song shown here because of the use of ledger lines, which will be introduced on a later chart.]

INTRODUCE THE CHART

1. Hold your hand over the hand signal for "mi" on the chart. Sing "mi" with the class with hand signals.
2. Point to the "re" on the chart. Tilt your hand so it points upward. Sing "re" with the class.
3. Make the hand signal for "do" on the chart and sing it with the class.
4. Repeat these activities, moving from one syllable to another in various patterns.
5. Use the hand and fingers to establish the position of "re" in relationship to "mi" and "do."

"If mi is here"

"Where is re?"

Later, use your hand to show the position of re in relationship to sol and la.

OTHER SONGS TO USE

"Mary Had a Little Lamb"
m r d r m m m

"Are You Sleeping?"
d r m d, d r m d

"Yankee Doodle"
d d r m d m r (s)

ADDITIONAL ACTIVITIES

[Note: The children have now learned the entire pentatonic scale (do, re, mi, sol, la). There are many songs written in the pentatonic, starting on low sol (s₁) and using low la (l₁). These songs can be taught by rote.]

1. Choose five children to represent the pentatonic scale, giving each one a tone syllable. This activity is sometimes called the human organ:

| do | re | mi | sol | la | do' |

Have each child hold a flash card of his tone syllable. Establish the pitch—either "sol" or "do." As you point to the syllables, the class sings with hand or arm signals. Move slowly from interval to interval. Ask one child to lead this activity.

[Note: This activity can only be accomplished successfully when the children are confident with the intervals that have been presented.]

2. The concept of larger instruments having lower voices can be demonstrated by choosing the tallest child to be low "do" and the smallest child to represent high "do."
3. Sing various patterns using notes of the pentatonic scale with hand signals. Class echoes.

Teacher sings   Class echoes

```
 |  |  ⊓  |        |  |  ⊓  |
 s  s  m r d       s  s  m r d

 |  |  |  ⅜        |  |  |  ⅜
 m  r  d           m  r  d
```

4. Use hand signals but *do not* sing. Then, have class sing the tone syllables with hand signals.

5. Make flash cards of various melodic patterns using re. Establish the pitch:

sol | ⊓ | | do ⊓ ⊓ | |
    s m r d d   d d r r m s

Hold up the card. Class sings with hand signals. Then, move from child to child and let individuals sing the patterns on the flash cards.

6. Put the musical staff on the chalkboard but have class use individual charts. Establish where the beginning note will be.

Teacher sings
with hand signals

```
 |  |  ⊓  |
 s  m  r  r  d

 ⊓  |  ⊓  |
 d  r  m  m  r  d
```

Class echoes
and writes

Choose individual children to come to the board and write the melodic pattern. This will give the children in the class an opportunity to correct their own mistakes.

7. Turn to Chart 40.

Hop Old Squirrel

4. Sing the song and draw a picture of the melody in the air with arms or fingers. Draw a picture of the melody on paper (each child's picture will vary).

INTRODUCE THE CHART

1. Ask one child to clap the rhythm pattern on the chart with rhythm syllables. (Only the last two phrases of the song are on the chart.)
2. Ask another child to keep the beat on the chart while the class reads and claps the rhythm pattern.
3. Sing the tone syllables on the chart with the class, using hand or arm signals.
4. Choose one child to sing the first and third lines of the chart (Hop old squirrel), and another child to sing the second and fourth lines (Eideldum). Use hand or arm signals.
5. Put the rhythm pattern of the *entire* song on the chalkboard (as it is written in the music).

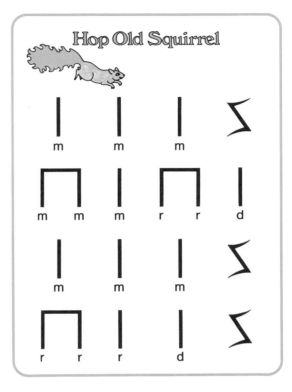

PREPARATION FOR THE CHART

1. Teach the song. (Only a portion of the song appears on the chart.)
2. Sing the song and use previous rhythmic experiences.
3. Sing the song, hop the "Hop old squirrel" pattern (| | | ⅔), and balance on one foot for "Eideldum." Create various motions for the song:

"Hop old squirrel"	"Eideldum"
jump	turn around
turn while hopping	arm motions
clap	step
step	finger motions

Encourage the children to change body motions on the beat.

American Folk Song

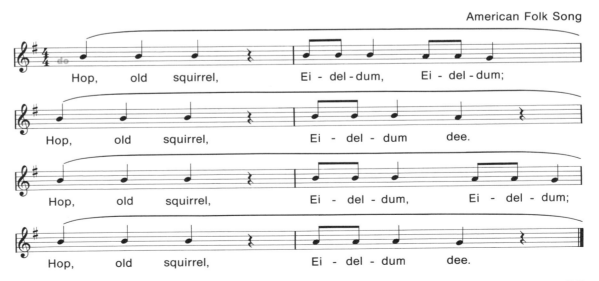

Hop, old squirrel, Ei - del - dum, Ei - del - dum;

Hop, old squirrel, Ei - del - dum dee.

Hop, old squirrel, Ei - del - dum, Ei - del - dum;

Hop, old squirrel, Ei - del - dum dee.

6. Sing the song with tone syllables, one line at a time. As the class sings one line, choose one child to write the letter names of the tone syllables under the rhythm pattern.

| | | ∳
m m m

Let the children discover the rhythm syllables for the fourth measure:

Ei-del-dum dee
𝅨 | | ∳
m m m r

Does it end on "do"?

OTHER SONGS TO USE

"Hot Cross Buns"
| | | ∳ | | | | ∳
m r d | m r d

"Button You Must Wander"
𝅨 𝅨 | |
d d d r m s

"My Lord, What a Morning"
| 𝅘𝅥 𝅨 | | ∳ ∳
m m r m | d d

Use these song fragments and other songs that have a mi–re–do pattern as mystery songs, using only hand signals and rhythm pattern.

ADDITIONAL ACTIVITIES

1. Draw two lines on the floor (mi–do). As the class sings the song slowly, let several children hop or jump the melodic pattern:

"Hot Cross Buns"

X X X ∳ X X X ∳

2. *Two hand singing*. Move your hands slowly from one note to another, giving the children an opportunity to hear the interval before they sing.

Two-hand singing (Sol–Mi)

- Divide the class into two groups.
- Tell one group to follow and sing the tone signals of your left hand, and the other group to follow your right hand. Begin on a unison syllable and move one hand at a time. Establish the pitch of the starting note.

L.H. s l s m d – – – – m s m d
R.H. s – – – d r m s m – – m d

[*Note: Keep the distance of each interval relative to the movement of your hands. Refer to the vertical scale on Chart 17 if necessary.*]

3. Turn to Chart 41.

Mystery Songs

PREPARATION FOR THE CHART

Are You Sleeping?

1. Teach the song.
2. Sing the song, using previous rhythmic experiences.
3. Sing the song with a melodic ostinato (e.g., sol–do on the first and third beats).
4. Sing the song as a round in two, three, or four parts, depending on the musical abilities of your class.
5. Sing the song as a round, step the beat, and turn the phrases.

French:

Frère Jacques, Frère Jacques,
Dormez-vous. Dormez-vous?
Sonnez les matines,
Sonnez les matines,
Din, din, don, Din, din, don.

French phonetic

Freh-ruh Zha-kuh, Freh-ruh Zha-kuh,
Dor-may voo, dor-may- voo?
Soh-nay-leh ma-tee-nuh, Soh-ney leh ma-tee-nuh.
Din, din, don, Din, din, don.

Spanish:

Fray Felipe, Fray Felipe,
Duermes tu, Duermes tu?
Toque la campana,
Toque la campana,
Tin, tan, ton, Tin, tan, ton.

Spanish phonetic

Fray Feh-lee-peh, Fray Feh-lee-peh,
Dwehr-mehs too? Dwehr-mehs too?
Toh-kah lah kahm-pah-na, Toh-kah lah kham-pah-na,
Teen, tahn, tohn, teen, tahn, tohn.

German:

Meister Jakob, Meister Jakob,
Schlafst du noch, Schlafst du noch?
Horst du nicht die Glocken,
Horst du nicht die Glocken?
Bim bam bum, Bim bam bum.

German phonetic

My-ster Yah-kohb, My-ster Yah-kohb,
Shlahfst do nohch, Shlahfst do nohch?
Herst do nihkt dee Glohk-ehn? Herst do nihkt
dee Glohk-ehn?
Bihm, bahm, bohm, Bihm, bahm, bohm.

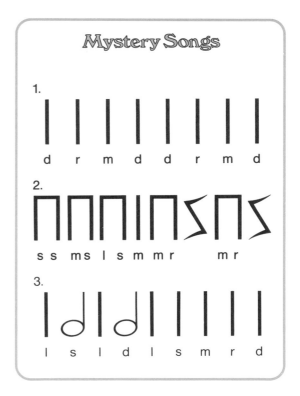

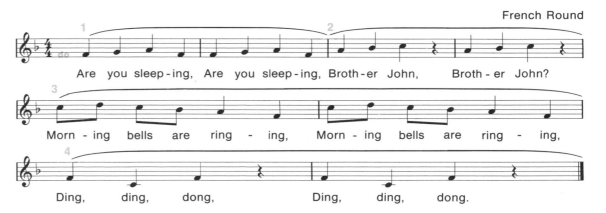

ARE YOU SLEEPING?

Camptown Races

1. Clap the rhythm pattern as a mystery song.
2. Create a rhythmic ostinato using various integrated motions to vary the sound:

| ⌐‾‾⌐ | | |
clap snap snap clap slap knees

[Note: This activity will require concentration and coordination. Begin with a simple pattern using repeated motions and progress to more complex motor activities.]

Goodbye, Old Paint

1. Teach the song. There are many verses to be found in folk songbooks or music textbooks.
2. The rhythmic activities will vary with this song because the beat is in three. Sing the song, sway back and forth to the pulse (one to the measure).
3. Sing the song, sway the pulse, step the beat (3).

  - How many steps did the children take to each "sway"? (3).
  - Does the song start on the first beat?
  - What is the name of the beat before 1? (anacrusis)

Stephen Foster — Chorus

Camp-town la - dies sing this song, / Goin' to run all night,
Doo - dah! Doo - dah! / Goin' to run all day! I'll
Camp-town race - track five miles long, / bet my mon-ey on a bob - tail nag,
Oh, Doo - dah - day! / Some bod - y bet on the bay.

GOODBYE, OLD PAINT

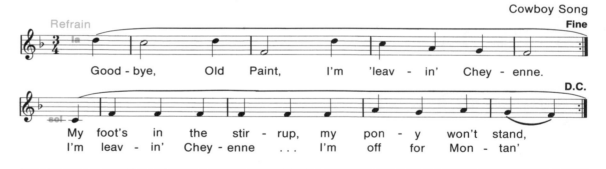

Cowboy Song

Good - bye, Old Paint, I'm 'leav - in' Chey - enne.
My foot's in the stir - rup, my pon - y won't stand,
I'm leav - in' Chey - enne . . . I'm off for Mon - tan'

INTRODUCE THE CHART

1. Clap one of the patterns on the chart. Let the class identify the pattern by number (1, 2, or 3). Ask the child who identified the pattern to sing the tone syllables with hand signals. Can the class identify the song? Sing the song, using hand signals for the phrase on the chart.

2. Continue through the chart.

  - Clap pattern
  - Identify the song
  - Sing the tone syllables with hand signals
  - Identify the song
  - Sing the song, using hand signals for the phrase on the chart.

3. "Goodbye, Old Paint" can be sung in its entirety with hand signals if you introduce the low "sol" by rote. (Use the vertical scale to show the relative position of the interval.)
4. Establish the starting pitch. Keep the beat on the chart, but *do not* sing. Now, ask the class to sing each phrase on the

chart with hand signals. Can they sing the chart alone? (Not all children will be successful with this activity.)

5. Establish the starting pitch. Make the hand signals for one of the phrases on the chart but *do not* sing. Have the class sing the phrase with syllables or words and hand signals.

ADDITIONAL ACTIVITIES

1. Use a rhythm pattern contained in one of the songs as an instrumental ostinato. Encourage musical discrimination. For example,

   "Are You Sleeping?"
   triangle: ⊓ ⊓ Ι Ι
   small woodblock: Ι Ι Ι Ι

   "Camptown Races"
   woodblock: ⊓ ⊓ ⊓ Ι
   tambourine: ⊓ ₹ ⊓ ₹

   "Goodbye, Old Paint"
   woodblock: Ι Ι ♩ Ι Ι ♩
   jingle bells: Ι Ι Ι Ι Ι Ι ♩

2. Sing, "Are You Sleeping?"

   • Choose one phrase to sing as a melodic ostinato.

• Combine melodic and instrumental ostinatos while one group sings the song.
• Play the melodic ostinato on the bells or recorder.

   Are you sleeping: C D E C
   Brother John: E F G
   Morning bells
     are ringing: ⊓ ⊓ Ι Ι
              GA GF E C
   Ding, ding, dong: Ι Ι Ι ₹
              C G C

This activity can be done with most rounds.

3. As the children become confident in performing ostinatos, let them create their own.

   • Establish a rhythm pattern.
   • Add tone syllables to the rhythm pattern.
   • Sing the melodic pattern.
   • Divide the class. One group sings the melody, the other group sings the ostinato.

[Note: This activity will require some experimentation with sound. Which intervals are pleasing to the ear and which intervals create a dissonance. Remember, dissonance is not always as unpleasant to children as it is to adults.]

4. Turn to Chart 42.

What Do You Hear?

[*Note: This chart will act as a culmination to the Level 1 charts. Several of the concepts will be presented for review.*]

PREPARATION FOR THE CHART

1. Ask the class: How many beats are there to a measure? (2)   What does the double bar tell you? (‖ —end of a song) What does the double bar with dots mean? (‖: :‖—repeat)
2. Review the position of the notes on the staff. "If sol is on the third line, where is la?" (space above sol or fourth space) Continue through the rest of the syllables.

INTRODUCE THE CHART

1. Choose one child to clap the rhythm pattern of one of the lines on the chart. Have the class identify the pattern. Continue through the chart.
2. Ask a volunteer to sing one of the lines on the chart with syllables and hand signals. If he is confident, let him establish his own starting pitch. The class will echo with tone syllables and hand signals, *only* if he is correct and observes all the symbols on the chart. If he is incorrect, the class will remain silent, and the child can either correct his mistake or choose another child.

3. Sing one of the lines of the chart on a neutral syllable (loo) with hand signals. The class will echo with tone syllables and hand signals. Can they identify which phrase it is on the chart?
4. Sing various lines on the chart sometimes *deliberately* altering either the rhythm pattern or some of the intervals. Tell the class they may echo if the rhythm pattern and melodic pattern is on the chart.

ADDITIONAL ACTIVITIES

1. Sing or play, on the bells or recorder, a melodic pattern using the pentatonic scale (do–re–mi–sol–la). Establish the

position of the starting note. The children will write the pattern on the staff. (This may be done on the chalkboard or individual staff charts.) Begin with one-measure patterns. Later, use two measures with more difficult rhythms.

Sing or play:

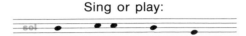

2. Choose individuals to sing a melodic pattern with hand signals using the pentatonic scale. The class will echo.

EVALUATION OF RHYTHMIC AND PERCEPTUAL SKILLS

EVALUATION OF RHYTHMIC AND PERCEPTUAL SKILLS

Psychomotor Development and Perception

1. Can the children feel the beat of the song with motor activities?

- stepping
- walking
- clapping
- swaying

2. Can they feel the phrase of the song with motor activities?
3. Can they make pictures of the melody, showing up and down position of the intervals and phrases?

Aural Acuity and Perception

1. Can the children hear and recognize the interval of the major second when it is played or sung within a familiar song? When played on an instrument?
2. Can they hear the interval of the major second with inner hearing while observing only hand signals?

Visual Acuity and Perception

1. Can the children recognize and sing the interval of the major second while reading and singing the charts?
2. Are they aware of the position of the intervals on the staff?

Brooms

Traditional Dutch Round

Brooms, brooms, brooms, brooms,

What are they for?   What are they for?

Sweep-ing,   sweep-ing,   sweep-ing,

sweep-ing   the floors,   floors.

3. Sing the song as a round in two, three, or four parts, depending on the ability of your class.
4. Step or walk the song as a round; singing and stepping the pattern, or stepping the pattern only, without singing.

PREPARATION FOR THE CHART

1. Teach the song. (This is an adaptation of an old Dutch round that can be found in many textbooks under the title "De Besom."
2. Sing the song and use previous rhythmic experiences. The children will enjoy stepping the rhythm pattern. Use flash cards to change the activities:

   clap—phrase one
   step—phrase two
   feel—phrase three
   sing—phrase four

INTRODUCE THE CHART

1. Read and clap the rhythm pattern with rhythm syllables.
2. Read and clap the rhythm pattern. Step the beat.
3. Clap the beat. Step the rhythm pattern.
4. Speak the words. Clap the beat. Step the rhythm pattern.
5. Review the "high do" tone syllable (do'—Chart 32.)
6. Read the chart but do not sing. Use arm signals for the tone syllables on each phrase, while keeping the beat.

7. Sing the song with arm signals and tone syllables.
8. Sing the song with arm signals and tone syllables. Dramatize the position of the intervals:

   "Brooms"—fists on the floor
   "What are they for"—slap the
     knees, rising slightly
   "Sweeping—stand up and clap hands
   "Floors"—fists over head.

9. Repeat the last activity using words.
10. Divide the class into two or three groups. Sing the song as a round and use body motions (activity 8).

ADDITIONAL ACTIVITIES

1. *Game:*

   - Equipment: A broom that is fairly new and stiff so when dropped will bounce straight up.
   - Formation: Circle, one child holding the broom in his right hand. Sing the song beginning slowly.
   - "Brooms, brooms"—bounce broom two times with right hand and pass quickly to left hand.
   - "Brooms"—bounce broom once with left hand.
   - "Brooms"—bounce and pass broom to person on the left without losing the beat.

   Continue singing the song, passing the broom on every fourth beat:

   | | | |
   R.H. R.H. L.H. pass,
   ⌢3 | ⌢3 |
   ∏ | ∏ |
   R.H. R.H. L.H. pass

   If one child drops the broom or loses the beat he must take his seat. Increase the tempo, getting faster on each repeat until the game ends with only two children remaining. (The class continues singing the song.)

2. A variation of this game is to choose four children to sing the song as a four-part round. The first child sings "Brooms, brooms, brooms, brooms," and passes the broom on the fourth beat, while continuing to sing the song. The second child sings "Brooms, brooms, brooms, brooms," and so on.

EVALUATION OF RHYTHMIC AND PERCEPTUAL SKILLS

Psychomotor Development and Perception

Are the children increasing their ability to coordinate various activities?

Musical Development and Social Maturity

Are the children approaching new activities with enthusiasm and enjoyment?

[Note: If you feel that the children are not successful while performing an activity, it would be wise to review previous charts. This will insure their success and add to their enjoyment.]

Rain, Rain, Go Away

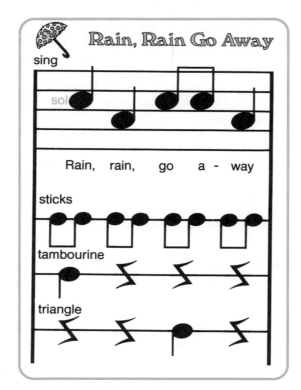

Rain, Rain Go Away

sing

sol

Rain,　rain,　　go　a - way

sticks

tambourine

triangle

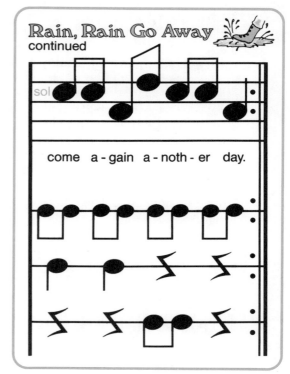

Rain, Rain Go Away

continued

sol

come　a - gain　a - noth - er　day.

PREPARATION FOR THE CHART

In this lesson we introduce score reading. When the staves are connected by a line on the left-hand side, they are all read and played, or sung, simultaneously. It is helpful and interesting to show the children an instrumental score, so they can see how the instrumental parts are written on a conductor's score.

INTRODUCE THE CHART

1. Establish the pitch for sol and sing the top line of both charts with the class. Use tone syllables and hand signals. Observe the repeat signs.

2. Sing the top line with words and hand signals.
3. Sing the top line of the chart with words and tap the beat on the desk.
4. Ask one child to clap the rhythm pattern of the second line of both charts while the class taps the beat softly.
5. Sing the song and tap the second line on the desk.
6. Choose one child to read and clap the third line of both charts, observing the rests and repeat signs. The class softly taps the beat and sings the song.
7. Repeat activity 6 for the last line of the chart.
8. Divide the class into four groups.

- Group 1—sings the song
- Group 2—taps the second line
- Group 3—claps the third line
- Group 4—raps (knuckles) the fourth line

Establish the beat by saying, "One, two, ready, sing"

9. Distribute the rhythm instruments to individual children (the orchestra). Establish the beat. Class sings the song, while individuals play the pattern on the charts.
10 Create words to the patterns on lines three and four:

Line 3:
Splash—❙ ❳ ❳ ❳ ❘ ❙ ❙ ❳ ❳ :❙❙

Line 4:
Drip, dribble—❳ ❳ ❙ ❳ ❘ ❳ ❳ ⊓ ❳ :❙❙

Divide the class into four groups. Sing the first line, tap the second line, and speak the words for lines three and four.

[Note: Not all children will be able to perform this highly integrated activity, but they will enjoy trying.]

ADDITIONAL ACTIVITIES

[Note: This song uses only notes contained within the pentatonic scale. Let the children create a two-measure melodic pattern using these tones.]

1. Choose one child to clap a two-measure rhythm pattern.

   - Put the pattern on the chalkboard.
   - Create a melody with tone syllables. Put the letters under the rhythm pattern:

   ❙❙: ❙ ❳ ⊓ ❙ ❙ ❙ ❙ ❳ :❙❙
     d   m m s ❙ s m

   - Create words to the melodic pattern

Rain coming down cold and gray.

   Divide the class. Group 1 sings the chart; Group 2 sings the original melody with words. Several original melodies can be used while one group sings the song.

2. Instruments, such as bells, piano, recorder, or song flute, can be used with activity 1. Create melodic patterns using notes of the pentatonic scale.

3. Use poetry suitable to the grade level.

- Discover and write the rhythm pattern of a poem on the chalkboard.
- Create a melody, using only sol–la–mi (chant).
- Create an accompaniment (instrumental ostinatos or melodic ostinatos with words).

EVALUATION AND SUMMARY

Psychomotor Development and Perception

1. Do the children have a strong feeling for the beat and rhythm pattern?
2. Do they perform integrated rhythmic activities with confidence?

   - singing–stepping or walking
   - singing–turning phrase
   - clapping pattern–stepping or walking the beat
   - clapping beat–stepping pattern
   - singing–tapping ostinato

Aural Acuity and Perception

1. Can the children hear the intervals within the pentatonic scale?

minor third:	sol–mi
major second:	sol–la
perfect fourth:	la–mi
major third:	mi–do
major second:	re–do
perfect fifth:	sol–do
octave:	do–do'

2. Can they hear and identify long and short sounds?

ta:	❙	quarter rest: ❳
ti–ti:	⊓	whole rest: ▬
ta–a:	♩	

Visual Acuity and Perception

1. Can the children read the tone and rhythm symbols on the chart with ease?
2. Can they discover the starting tone when "sol" or "do" is given on the staff?
3. Can they read simple songs containing do–re–mi–sol–la?

Musical Development and Social Maturity

1. Do the children participate and contribute with enthusiasm, involvement, and the beginnings of musical discrimination?
2. Do they identify similarities and differences?
3. Do they derive personal satisfaction from their musical achievement?
4. Are they beginning to think musically at their own level?
5. Are they aware of beats in two or three?
6. Are they able to exercise some musical discrimination:

   - dynamics (loud and soft)
   - appropriate instruments
   - appropriate tempo of song
   - differences in tone quality

7. Do they show an increasing willingness to listen and participate?

Hand Signals

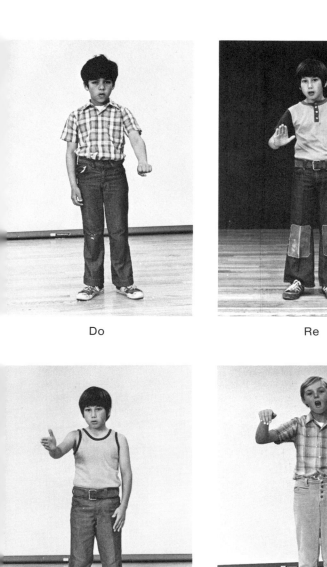

Do

Re

Mi

Fa

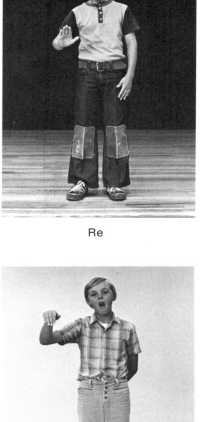

Sol

La

Ti

Do'